Developing
Professional Skills:
SECURED TRANSACTIONS

Martha M. Ertman

Carole & Hanan Sibel Research Professor
University of Maryland Carey Law School

Series Editor: Colleen Medill

WEST
ACADEMIC
PUBLISHING

© 2018 LEG, Inc. d/b/a West Academic
444 Cedar Street, Suite 700
St. Paul, MN 55101
1-877-888-1330

West, West Academic Publishing, and West Academic are trademarks of West Publishing Corporation, used under license.

Printed in the United States of America
ISBN: 978-1-68328-368-3

Table of Contents

Preface with Acknowledgments
DPS: Secured Transactions

UNTIL A FEW YEARS AGO, most law faculty—myself included—assumed that law firms would train our graduates how to read, draft, and revise a contract once they were on the job. But then the firms, the American Bar Association, and some state bar associations began to press law schools to better prime students for practice. Wanting to give my students a leg up in a job market that was particularly tight, I began to integrate transactional skills into my contracts and commercial law courses. Over several years I developed two and three-credit courses in contract drafting and a 1-credit add-on drafting workshop to secured transactions. Looking back, I can hardly believe that it took me so long to realize how working with the actual agreements helps students understand legal doctrines and also demonstrates to employers a basic familiarity with the terminology and logistics of transactional practice. Now I believe that every student should graduate from law school knowing the difference between a representation and a covenant, and how to craft a materiality or knowledge qualifier to allocate risk between parties. With every set of contracts I assign and grade—letters of intent; employment agreements; bills of sale; promissory notes; and security agreements—I become more convinced that every contract-related course can and should include this essential material.

As I developed the materials that became this book, the ABA debated then adopted new transition-to-practice rules that require every graduate of an accredited law school to take six credits of experiential coursework. Law clinics and trial practice classes offer litigation simulations, but they rarely engage transactional issues. This book aims to fill that gap by giving law students experience negotiating, reading, drafting, and editing a simple set of contracts, getting feedback along the way so that they and the professors can assess their progress. At the end of the course each student will have a portfolio that can serve as a writing sample demonstrating facility with transactional work. Law schools, in turn, can use this curriculum to ensure that learning outcomes include the three core skills necessary for a transactional practice: (1) understanding a business transaction; (2) translating its terms into contract concepts like representations, warranties, and covenants; and (3) combining these two to reduce a negotiated agreement to words on the page.

Getting this book reduced to words on a page required contributions from many sharp minds. First and foremost is Prof. Olivia Farrar of Howard University Law School, an expert in contract negotiation and drafting who generously shared her expertise and time with me and with the students at the University of Maryland Carey Law School when she and I co-taught my first contract drafting and negotiation class. The UM Carey deans made that collaboration possible through their support for pedagogical experiment as well as a 1-credit add-on to my Secured Transactions class that I developed from lessons learned in that first drafting course. Finally, the law school generously provided the research and administrative support necessary to turn these pedagogical lessons into this book.

My outstanding colleagues also contributed greatly. In contracts and business law, Michael Van Alstine, Michelle Harner (now a U.S. Bankruptcy Judge in the District of Maryland), and Jana Singer gave freely of their time and teaching and practice expertise, served as sounding boards, proofread chapters, and in Michael's case, tried out one of these exercises in his own commercial law class. Other colleagues—Deb Eisenberg, Sheldon Krantz, and Barbara Bezdek— helped me structure negotiation exercises and provided expertise in legal ethics and clinical pedagogy. Law librarians Sue McCarty and Susan Herrick tracked down statutes and forms in record time and with extraordinary precision. Administrative assistants

Shyala Rumsay and Frank Lancaster compiled materials into a coherent whole, often on a short timeline to get students draft chapters before each class.

UM law students beta tested the materials in my Fall 2016 contract drafting class, and four of them agreed to allow their work to be featured in the teacher's manual as samples of student work for each assignment: Alina Chernin, Olamide Orebamjo, George Cunningham, and Christopher Cook. All of these students, and those in prior semesters, helped iron out wrinkles from earlier iterations of these exercises.

In addition, student research assistants carefully proofread each chapter of the book and teacher's manual, conducted research, and provided helpful feedback to make the voice, format and substance of this book accessible to students and also in-depth and professional. Many thanks to Kimberly Foerster, Ben Fuld, Emily Gallin, Ben Ofori, Matt Sarna, Rosy Shrestha, and Ashton Zylstra for these contributions, and most of all to Angela Lam, who coordinated these reviewers and provided outstanding research, administrative, and editorial support as both a TA and RA.

A project that seeks to help law schools better prepare their students for practice required guidance from the world beyond the legal academy. Experts in banking, commercial law, and law school publishing helped this book accurately represent a typical secured transaction that works for both seasoned and new law school faculty: Alissa Curry Briggs, Carol McGeehan, Colleen Medill, Louis Higgins, Pamela Siege Chandler, Staci Herr, David Lash, Carlie Wells, Mark Winston, Michele Zavos, and the editors at West Academic. Anne Stom gave me the excellent example of a hardware store, a minimally-regulated business that is familiar to every law student. Leading commercial law teachers Lynn LoPucki and Robert Lawless provided comments on early iterations, and David Hague and Bruce Markell provided additional feedback from the trenches of commercial law teaching. I am grateful to them all.

Thanks too to Thomas Haggard, George Kuney and Billy Sjostrom for their permission to use their books on legal writing, from which I have excerpted a good bit of the text that explains contract drafting terminology and techniques.

Finally, thanks to my family for listening patiently to stories about all these interactions over the dinner table, and cheerfully supporting me through the challenges of updating pedagogical techniques at the midpoint of my law teaching career. My son Oscar inspires me to try new things, and his dad Victor Flatt—also a law professor— shared his own experiences of integrating experiential elements to environmental law classes. The biggest family contribution to this book is my wife Karen Lash's expertise in bringing the real world into law school life, which has changed the way I see law, write about it, and teach it. Indeed, our daily conversations led me to believe that contracts and commercial law teachers have an ethical obligation to include basic instruction on reading and editing contracts in our classes. I wrote this book to help others meet that goal.

Introduction
Overview

THIS BOOK REINFORCES doctrinal material in a commercial law course by providing students hands-on experience with the documents that memorialize a secured transaction. It is designed to be used as a supplement to the leading Secured Transactions casebooks (or survey commercial law casebooks in the same series) but can be adapted to most commercial law casebooks.[1] Consistent with variations in law school curricula as course offerings evolve to incorporate more transition-to-practice materials, this book can be used within a doctrinal course, as the text for a drafting workshop appended to a commercial law course, or in a stand-alone drafting class. Each format provides students with knowledge that is essential to a transactional practice.

The book uses a simulation based on a real-life successful business transaction: the financed purchase of a hardware store. This familiar context—just about everyone has bought a hammer or paint from a hardware store—provides a platform for students to master new material. Learning to read, negotiate, and draft the documents necessary to create the specialized contracts that define this transaction will help you better understand legal doctrine by applying it in a variety of documents and also develop the foundational skills of transactional attorneys.

---

1   The Secured Transactions casebooks are Lynn Lopucki, Elizabeth Warren & Robert Lawless, *Secured Credit: A Systems Approach* (8th ed. 2016); Linda J. Rusch & Stephen L. Sepinuck, *Problems & Materials on Secured Transactions* (4th ed. 2017); William D. Warren & Steven D. Walt, *Secured Transactions in Personal Property* (9th ed. 2013); and Douglas J. Whaley & Stephen M. McJohn, *Problems & Materials on Secured Transactions* (9th ed. 2014).

Because learning to write in a new format requires repetition and feedback, these exercises provide repeated opportunities to develop the skills of problem solving, negotiation, drafting, and complying with ethical obligations. By the end of the course, you should be able to read and understand a contract as well as negotiate and draft concise, coherent, legally binding contracts that reflect the business deal entered by the parties.

These exercises are modular. Your professor may assign all of them or select the ones that work with the class format. In addition to this book, you have access to this book's website (www.developingskills. com) and may also receive handouts from your professor. The website includes downloadable sample documents that you can use as templates for your drafts as well as other agreements that would be included in this transaction but are beyond the scope of this course.

As a whole, the exercises develop skills in three core competencies required in a transactional law practice: (1) understanding a client's business deal; (2) translating those terms to contract concepts like definitions, representations, warranties and covenants; and (3) translating those concepts to words on the page that legally bind the parties. In addition to these transferrable skills, at the end of the course, you will have created legally binding documents that memorialize the transaction, which may be useful as a writing sample in your job search.

The documents you will negotiate and draft each serve a function in the financed sale of Urban Hardware:

1. <u>Promissory Note</u>: memorializes the debtor's debt to the bank

2. <u>Security Agreement</u>: protects the bank by creating a link between the debtor's property and the debt

3. <u>Personal Guaranty</u>: protects the bank by making Bianca Bolt personally liable for some or all of the debtor's debt

4. <u>Financing Statement</u>: perfects the bank's security interest in the collateral

5. <u>Notice of Lien</u>: perfects the bank's security interest in the debtor's truck

Your professor may assign just exercises #1–4 to have students create a bare-bones perfected security interest, with no bells or whistles. In the alternative, your class may add on exercises #5 and #6 to provide students with an opportunity to work with representations, warranties, covenants, and endgame provisions, which security agreements typically include. For courses that include a more intensive drafting experience, exercises #7 and #9 add a personal guaranty and perfection for certificate of title goods and fixtures. Exercise #8 works with any of the exercises to enrich students' understanding of professional ethics in transactional work by introducing an ethical dilemma to the simulation. Finally, exercise #10 provides a capstone experience by having you compile the full portfolio of documents and write a memo to the client explaining how the security interest was perfected.

Administration:

▶ **Teams:**

Law practice requires collaboration, and students often produce better work and learn more if they team up. Moreover, contracts require two parties to negotiate with each other. Consequently, these exercises are designed for pairs of students, with one playing the role of the debtor's attorney and the other playing the role of the bank's attorney. After a brief, structured negotiation exercise, each team submits its assignment for a single grade.

▶ **Exercise Format:**

The exercises each contain the following:

- *Overview:* The subtitle of each exercise specifies the skill it covers and the exercise begins by providing basic information to explain its purpose and content. It describes the role of the document being drafted within the transaction as a whole and identifies discrete parts of the business transaction that you will negotiate then commit to words on the page.

- *Contract Drafting & Negotiation Essentials*: Each exercise explains then applies the essential contract drafting issues. If the exercise involves negotiation, it provides basic information on a negotiation technique, then applies it as student teams negotiate the terms of the document.

- *Legal Rules*: Prior to drafting, students are reminded of the relevant sections of UCC Article 9 and any other statutes or rules.

- *Student Assignment*: Most of the exercises involve the use of a sample agreement used in a similar transaction. Just as transactional attorneys edit a template—sometimes called a "precedent" or "exemplar"—you will edit a document from a similar transaction to make it match the transaction between Bolt's Urban Hardware and First National Bank. The templates in this book were used in a successful transaction similar to the one here. Yet like many precedents they can be improved. Transactional attorneys fine-tune the terms of templates as they gain expertise in an area and learn how particular language can help or hinder a client's objectives. Accordingly, some of the assignments require you to edit the document to increase clarity, concision, practicality, and readability.

The remainder of this chapter sets out the facts of the hypothetical transaction.

Hypothetical

Bianca Bolt ("Bolt") is the manager of a hardware store doing business under the trade name Urban Hardware ("Urban Hardware" or "the Store"). The Store is located in a walking neighborhood of the city of Springfield. Prior to working at Urban Hardware, Bolt owned and operated a successful construction business. She took the job as manager to learn the business because she has long dreamed of owning a hardware store that is also a community hub, with a bike repair clinic, classes on planting for urban gardens, and other features. The Store's current owner, Sam Seller ("Seller") hired Bolt knowing that he was going to retire soon. He plans to sell the Store to Bolt for $1,000,000.

Bolt plans to use a $400,000 inheritance to pay part of the purchase price, and must borrow money to finance the remaining $600,000. First National Bank of Springfield ("FNB" or "the Bank") has loaned money to Bolt in past business transactions and is willing to finance the purchase of Urban Hardware.

Bolt plans to continue doing business under the name "Urban Hardware" because the Store has considerable goodwill and a sizeable customer base. Seller operated the Store as a sole proprietorship, but Bolt prefers to do business as a limited liability company, or LLC. She formed a single member LLC to acquire the assets of Urban Hardware and to operate it after the sale. The LLC's Articles of Organization—the charter that establishes the LLC's existence—list the LLC's name as "Bolt's Urban Hardware, LLC" ("the LLC" or "Bolt's Urban Hardware"). The Articles also identify Bolt as the Debtor's Managing Member.

Bolt transferred her $400,000 inheritance to the LLC so that the LLC could purchase Urban Hardware.[2] FNB requires that the loan for the remaining purchase price have three essential elements:

- the LLC must own all assets of the Store;

- a promissory note must memorialize the loan; and

- the promissory note must be secured by a perfected security interest in the Store's property (including income received in the future).

The following documents will meet these requirements and make the transaction legally binding between the parties:

- a promissory note (exercise #1)

- a UCC-1 Financing Statement (exercise #3)

- a security agreement (exercises #2 & #4, #5, and #6).[3]

---

[2] The LLC formally consented to the purchase of Urban Hardware in a document titled "Action of the Member of Bolt's Urban Hardware, LLC." That document establishes the LLC's authority to enter the transaction and is posted as a supplemental document on the book website.

[3] Your course may make the assignment conform more closely to a typical financed sale by including a personal guaranty and perfection of certificate of title goods and fixtures. Exercises #7 and #9 cover these issues.

FNB produced this Term Sheet that provides the core business provisions of the transaction.

TERM SHEET FOR FINANCED ASSET PURCHASE

BOLT'S URBAN HARDWARE d/b/a URBAN HARDWARE (DEBTOR) and
FIRST NATIONAL BANK OF SPRINGFIELD (LENDER)

TRANSACTION: Financing Debtor's Purchase of Urban Hardware, a hardware store located at 100 Industrial Way, Springfield, NY 13333[4] from Sam Seller

BORROWER: Bolt's Urban Hardware, LLC
100 Industrial Way
Springfield, NY 13333

Att'n: Bianca Bolt, Managing Member

LENDER: First National Bank of Springfield
700 N. Burns St.
Springfield Heights, NY 13333

FNB is a New York corporation

Att'n: Lamar Lee, Senior Vice President
of Commercial Lending

PERSONAL GUARANTOR: Bianca Bolt
742 Evergreen Terrace
Springfield, NY 13333

---

4   Your professor may tailor the exercises to another state. Except in exercise #3 on financing statements and #9 on certificate of title goods and fixtures, the state can be altered without affecting the rest of the exercises.

AMOUNT BORROWED:$600,000–800,000, to be negotiated

TERM: 10 years

INTEREST RATE: 5%[5]

COLLATERAL: All or most of the Store's property, to be negotiated

PAYMENTS: Monthly

DUE DATE: First of each month, but negotiable

OTHER CONDITIONS: To be specified in future exercises on basic and endgame provisions of the Security Agreement

You will pair off to negotiate and draft the documents in role, with one student playing the attorney for Bolt's Urban Hardware, LLC and the other playing the attorney for the First National Bank of Springfield.

The Store's property includes the following:

- inventory such as ladders, hammers, garden supplies, etc.;

- equipment such as shelves, display cases, a paint-mixing machine, a key cutter, and cash registers that include terminals for customers to insert credit cards;

---

5 Interest rates are often tagged to the "prime rate," the interest rate that banks charge their best customers, which likely have strong credit ratings. The *Wall Street Journal* lists the prime rate: http://online.wsj.com/mdc/public/page/2_3020-moneyrate.html. An interest rate such as "prime plus 2%" would require that the drafter specify the date when prime is set, and any time it is altered (i.e., anually).

- heavy equipment that the Store leases to its customers for major home and lawn projects such as refinishing floors, vacuuming up water, power washing, and rototilling a lawn;

- A 10-year lease covering the building where Urban Hardware is located;

- A business checking account for "Bolt's Urban Hardware d/b/a Urban Hardware;"

- A bright orange logo, Urban Hardware®, which is well-known throughout Springfield; and

- Licenses and permits issued by the city and state for sales tax collection and business operation.

In addition, Bianca Bolt has an extensive inventory of vintage and antique wrought iron balconies, hinges, and knobs for doors and cabinetry ("antique ironwork"). Some of the antique ironwork is stored off-site with a storage firm that has issued a "warehouse receipt" confirming ownership by "Bianca Bolt."

The assets other than the antique ironwork are worth at least $800,000, a fact confirmed by independent appraisers. Adding in the antique ironwork could increase the value of the collateral to as much as $1,000,000.

A Note on Font, Templates, Supplemental Reading, and the Hypothetical

In addition to the material in this book, your professor may hand out sample documents, negotiation worksheets, and other documents. The templates used in exercises are posted in downloadable form on the book's website. In addition, students who are interested in understanding the full transaction—such as a bill of sale from Seller to Bolt's Urban Hardware—can access those documents on the website.

The readings on contract drafting and negotiation skills featured in this book are excerpted from leading materials on the subject. They have been edited to focus on secured transactions and to standardize the material with the rest of this book. Of necessity they are short and convey only foundational information on the relevant provisions you are working on. Once you establish that foundation, you can refine your transactional knowledge and skills in future courses and in your law practice. Books that supplement the material here include the following texts on drafting: ; Charles M. Fox, *Working with Contracts* (2d ed. 2008); Thomas R. Haggard & George W. Kuney, *Legal Drafting: Process, Techniques and Exercises* (2d ed. 2007) and 2017 (3d. ed with Donna C. Looper); George W. Kuney, *The Elements of Contract Drafting* (4th ed. 2014); Stephen L. Sepinuck and John Francis Hilson, *Transactional Skills* (2015); William K. Sjostrom, Jr., *An Introduction to Contract Drafting* (2d ed. 2013); and Tina Stark, *Drafting Contracts* (2d ed. 2014). Leading books on negotiation include Roger Fisher, William L. Ury & Bruce Patton, *Getting to Yes* (2d ed. 1991) and Deborah M. Kolb & Judith Williams, *Everyday Negotiation* (2003).

The hypothetical sale of Urban Hardware is fictional, as are Bianca Bolt, Lamar Lee, First National Bank, and all other characters. While a few names and addresses in exercise #3 come from the UCC-1 files to facilitate a search through the files for competing claims to collateral, any resemblance between these facts and real life is coincidental.

Developing Professional Skills:

SECURED
TRANSACTIONS

Promissory Note

Skill: Reading and Negotiating Contracts

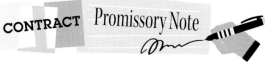

Overview

THIS EXERCISE introduces you to the core business transaction at the heart of most secured transactions: a loan. The documentation of that loan is a promissory note, which should look familiar if you borrowed money for undergraduate or law school tuition. If you are one of the many students who signed that note without fully understanding the rights and duties it establishes, then completing this exercise should greatly enrich your appreciation.

Keep in mind that a promissory note is just one type of loan agreement. When you use a VISA credit card, the agreement you sign when you applied for the card governs the lending relationship (supplemented by regulations that are covered in payments courses that address UCC Articles 3 and 4). Most credit card transactions are unsecured loans, while this course focuses on a secured loan. Many creditors insist on two documents in addition to the note to get preferential treatment over unsecured creditors: the security agreement and the financing statement. The security agreement creates a link between the debt and some of the debtor's property (collateral), and the financing statement increases the chance that the creditor's claims to the collateral will have priority over competing claimants.

As with each exercise in this book, this chapter alternates between explanations and applications. That format mimics the apprenticeship model traditionally used in medical school, in which students watch a procedure like drawing blood, do it themselves, then teach a fellow student how to perform it. While this see-one-do-one-teach-one model is not a perfect fit for legal education—and indeed has its critics within

1

medical education—the basic framework of having students learn a short lesson then apply it primes students for practice by supplementing the traditional law school march through cases and statutes.

These exercises teach you to distinguish the core elements of a contract that make it legally binding from satellite terms that are common and helpful but less likely to cause legal catastrophe if a drafter messes them up. You will come to understand how a transactional lawyer anticipates things that could go wrong and then negotiates and drafts to either prevent them or decrease the harms that flow from negative circumstances like missed payments, administrative errors, or debtor fraud.

Clients pay attorneys hundreds of dollars an hour to use these practice skills of planning, negotiation, drafting, and compliance with legal rules, so potential employers should be interested in seeing the portfolio of documents that result from doing the exercises in this book. Less obviously but just as importantly, completing these exercises helps to demonstrate your acquisition of professionalism, a core attribute of practicing lawyers. Taking professional pride in producing work product that both protects a client's interests and conforms to the expectations of business people and attorneys in its format and precision is among the most valuable skills acquired by completing these exercises.

Part I outlines the anatomy of a contract and the concepts that shape its terms then has you apply that knowledge by identifying the parts of a template promissory note. (Spoiler alert: you will use the same template in the drafting part of the exercise.) Part II returns to explication mode with material on the two major approaches to negotiation, which you then apply by negotiating the amount of the loan with the "attorney" for the other party. Part III briefly notes the relevant legal doctrines that shape promissory notes. It all comes together in Part IV, where you and your partner synthesize all this material by editing the template to reflect the details of your transaction.

Part I: Drafting Essentials[1]

A. Anatomy of a Contract Explained

Contract drafting is an important skill for any attorney and indispensable for a transactional attorney.[2] The skill takes time to develop through drafting and reviewing contracts. This introduction discusses some basic concepts of contract drafting to help you develop this important skill. At the end is an exercise to apply and expand the covered concepts.

Contract drafting is a unique type of writing. While the objective of most legal writing is either to persuade or convey information, neither of these objectives is the primary goal of a contract. The primary goal of a contract is to set forth the terms of the contracting parties' agreement in language that will be interpreted by all subsequent readers in exactly the same way. An attorney achieves that goal through precise and clear drafting.

The typical contract consists of the following parts:

- Title

- Preamble

- Recitals

---

1   Material in this section on contract drafting is based on Thomas R. Haggard and George W. Kuney, *Legal Drafting: Process, Techniques and Exercises*, 31–38; 314–315 42–43 (2d ed. 2007) and William K. Sjostrom, Jr., *An Introduction to Contract Drafting* 1–2 ; 41–43; 7–9 ; 14–15 and 11–12 ; 15–16 (2d ed. 2013).

2   A transactional attorney (also called a corporate attorney) works on transactions or deals such as mergers, acquisition, supply agreements, services agreements, and equipment leases. A transactional attorney advises the client as to the best way to structure a deal, negotiates the legal terms of the deal, and drafts or reviews the contract(s) to document the deal.

- Words of Agreement, often including a statement of consideration

- Definitions

- Core substantive provisions, including representations, warranties, covenants, conditions, and declarations

- Events of default and remedies

- Boilerplate

- Signature blocks

- Exhibits and attachments

The overall organization of a transactional document or group of transactional documents follows a group of rules:

- General provisions before specific ones

- Important, central provisions before others

- Rules before exceptions

- Separate provisions or sub-sections for each concept

- Technical, boilerplate, housekeeping, and miscellaneous provisions located last, before the signature blocks

B. How the Elements Work

Each element of a contract performs a specific function, as described below.

1. Title

Generally, begin the first page of any transactional document with a title in all caps, centered, and in bolded type. The title should identify the type of contract using a generic term, such as "Lease," "Prenuptial Agreement," or "Asset Purchase Agreement." For example, **RESIDENTIAL LEASE, CONTRACT OF SALE**, or **EMPLOYMENT CONTRACT.**

2. Preamble

The first paragraph of the agreement —often called the preamble— identifies the parties by their full legal names and the type of transaction they are documenting, indicates the terms that the contract will use when referring to both the document and the parties, and provides a date for the document. Ensure that all parties' names and other information (such as state of incorporation) are correct.

The preamble includes just this information. Other details belong in the recitals and the body of the contract.

The preamble can also include the addresses of the parties, as follows:

> *This Asset Purchase Agreement (**"APA"**) dated September 21, 2017, is between Mayfield & Associates, LLC, a Delaware limited liability company located at 100 Chicago Ave., Springfield IL, 62703 (**"Buyer"**) and Bronson Construction, Inc., a California corporation located at 100 Sacramento St., Springfield, CA 95370 (**"Seller"**).*

Note the form used to define a term. These defined terms should be used consistently throughout the document. To ease use of this agreement as a template for future transactions, choose generic defined terms like "Buyer," "Seller," "Landlord," "Tenant," etc. Then you can change of party name in the first paragraph rather than insert the new name every time the agreement refers to that party.

3. Recitals

Recitals set the context for the agreement and help with later interpretation. They also provide a place to list related transactional documents and other things that may be part of the transaction as a whole but are otherwise not referenced in the agreement itself. Recitals do not need to be preceded by the word "whereas" and is not necessary to title the section "Recitals," although you will no doubt run into those forms in practice (and those who aggressively adhere to them).

The recitals section explains why the parties entered the contract. Some courts have stated that recitals are not part of the contract. This is not correct. Recitals are as much a part of the contract as everything else in the document. The difference is that recitals are not promissory in form; they are statements of fact or belief. However, they serve other important functions and should be drafted with care. Each recital should be written in plain English, meaning that it is easy to understand and avoids overly complex vocabulary and legalese. These recitals should be preceded by a capital letter numbering or ordinal system (just like this section of this text). In the recitals, include facts that will help a later reader grasp the nature and purpose of the agreement.

A recital's explanation of the contract's purpose could be important if one of the parties later tries to avoid the contract under the doctrine of frustration of purpose. Or a recital might state a mutual understanding of fact, which could later pave the way for avoidance of the contract under the doctrine of mutual mistake. Facts stated as a recital might also be relevant to whether a breach qualifies as a material breach, since the recital will establish what is important to the parties. For example, if a particular brand of pipe is important to the owner of a house being constructed, then the recital could indicate this and explain why. If the body of the contract contains a "time is the essence" clause, you could include a recital that demonstrates why time is so important. Neither the clause nor the recital will ensure that the courts treat lateness as a material breach, but these provisions will certainly help.

Recitals are powerful medicine. Some courts have held that recitals are conclusive evidence of the facts they state. Recitals often provide background information that becomes relevant in the computation of damages. For example, a contract recital might list the profits that the enterprise has enjoyed over a certain period, thus easing proof of damages in the form of lost profits. Examples of appropriate facts for recitals include: (i) the relationship and goals of the parties; (ii) the nature of the transaction; and (iii) other transactional documents and things associated with the transaction. Take care to be accurate and not include unnecessary facts in the recitals—they may be used later in litigation to prove that which they state. When in doubt, be more general than specific in the recitals. Avoid the temptation to recite everything.

An appropriately drafted recital may also prevent a contract from being declared unconscionable for either procedural or substantive reasons. If a particular provision could appear to a judge to be harsh or unfair to one of the parties, and thus subject to a later unconscionability challenge, the recital could explain why the provision was included and indicate that the apparently disfavored party fully understands its implications.

Recitals do not contain obligations or promises. If an assertion of fact is unilateral, and is in essence a warranty by one of the parties, then it should be in the substantive sections of the contract with other warranties and be correctly labeled.

4. Words of Agreement and Statement of Consideration

Most contracts include words of agreement and a statement of consideration near the beginning of an agreement. Examples include the following[3] (which range from archaic and legalistic to plain English):

> *NOW, THEREFORE, premises considered and in consideration of the mutual covenants and agreements hereinafter set forth and in consideration of one dollar ($1.00) paid by Seller to Buyer, the receipt and adequacy whereof is hereby acknowledged, Seller and Buyer hereby covenant and agree as follows:*
>
> —or—
>
> *In consideration of the mutual promises set forth in this Agreement, the parties agree [as follows]:*
>
> —or—
>
> *[Accordingly] The Parties agree:*

The second formulation is preferable to the first or third, as it retains the notion of agreement and bargain and transitions a reader from the recital to the main body of the agreement. Further, it strips out all the excess verbiage that seems to elevate form over substance by suggesting that this recital of consideration will make the contract enforceable even if it is not true. Although this may be correct in limited circumstances—option contracts (*Restatement (Second) of Contracts* § 87), for example—the law is not uniform in this regard, and the lengthy chant about consideration may give false courage, a sort of whistling in the dark while walking by a graveyard. Better is the short statement of agreement that follows a recital that describes the transaction, including

3 Bracketed—[ ]—text in examples is optional language or language needing replacement when drafting a specific provision. Brackets should be deleted when using these provisions.

the bargained for nature of the exchange of covenants and other provisions that can aid in interpretation or demonstrate consideration.

5. Definitions

Transactional attorneys use the term "declaration" for a factual statement that the parties agree upon, like a stipulated fact in a lawsuit. Defined terms are one type of declaration, as are choice of law and other so-called boilerplate provisions that we will discuss below. Defined terms in an agreement essentially provide a private dictionary to tell a reader what a term means in this document. They are powerful tools that can decrease the length and increase the readability of substantive provisions. They allow you to lay out the full meaning of a complicated concept that must be addressed without cluttering the substantive provisions with litanies of near-synonymous terms. At the same time, they increase the readability of your document. In the same way that nicknames can make it easier to refer to a person, defined terms simplify reference longer, more detailed concepts.

For example, one definition of the word "claim" might be:

> *Any right to payment, whether or not such right is reduced to judgment, or is liquidated, fixed, contingent, matured, disputed, legal, equitable, or secured, or any right to an equitable remedy for breach or performance, whether or not such right to an equitable remedy is reduced to judgment, fixed, contingent, matured, disputed, or secured.*

If this definition is provided for separately in the document, the single word "Claim" can be used when needed in the contract's substantive provisions. Then its broad meaning is included without need for the litany. The initial capital letter ("Claim") tells the reader that it means the expansive definition set out above.

This example raises another issue, because this definition was taken from the Bankruptcy Code, specifically 11 U.S.C. § 101 (5). If there is a body of law that covers the concept you are trying to express, consider incorporating this law into your contract. In doing so, you must consider the effects of future amendments or repeals of the statute. Should you define the term with a reference to the citation of the statute alone? Or would your contract be more effective with a recitation of the current statutory definition because the citation will likely change? In any event, you could include the phrase, "as it may be amended from time to time."

Terms may be defined throughout the contract—in context—or in a stand-alone definitions section. Contextual definitions are especially appropriate for terms that appear only in one section or group of sections. If a term is used more widely or if the contract has many defined terms, provide a defined term section. Most drafters place this private dictionary for what specialized terms mean in a contract at the beginning of the contract, after the recitals and statement of consideration. Some, however, prefer to put it at the end, to be used as an index. For easy reference, put definitions in alphabetical order.

6. Substantive Provisions

This is the main body of the contract and contains the promises that each party has made. Tightly organize these provisions so that everything dealing with a particular aspect of the transaction is brought together in one place. Informative headings and sub-headings and proper outlining techniques make it easier to read and understand.

Five basic types of provisions provide the rights and duties of most contracts: representations and warranties, covenants, conditions, and endgame provisions. These basic building blocks of contracts, covered in depth in Chapters 4 to 6, are the mechanisms that give the contract substance. Representations and warranties capture statements of fact made by one party and relied upon by another party, covenants establish rights and duties of the parties, and conditions establish what happens if an event does or doesn't happen. Promissory notes, leases, security agreements, and other contracts that govern continuing relationships also feature endgame provisions that identify what counts as breach and its consequences, including dispute resolution issues like choice of law.

Lawyers pay particularly close attention to endgame provisions because at the front end of the deal—the negotiation and documentation stages—clients are primarily focused on performance, not on default. Endgame provisions appear at the end of a contract both to reflect parties' inclination to avoid thinking about the deal falling apart, and to mirror the chronology of the deal, since endgame become relevant at the end of the contractual relationship.

Exercise #6 focuses on endgame provisions in depth. Here we cover just one kind of provision that appears at the end of an agreement, interpretive clauses that are often dubbed "boilerplate."

7. Boilerplate or Housekeeping Provisions

These provisions deal generally with the administration of the contract. Some of them, but not all, are known as boilerplate. The term "boilerplate" is derived from the word for flat-rolled steel used to make steam engine boilers and the hulls of ships. In the early days of newspaper syndication, the term was also used to describe the plates of non-movable type that publishers delivered to local newspapers. It contained the syndicated text and advertising that the local paper would adopt in full, adding its own stories and advertising to supplement the syndicator's standard material. The term was first used in the legal context in the mid-1950s, as reference to standard clauses found in most contracts. That is the salient characteristic of good boilerplate—it contains language that allows it to be used in a variety of documents.

Unfortunately, many people, lawyers and non-lawyers, believe in the inviolability of the wording of whatever boilerplate they are familiar with, however hoary with age the verbiage might be. This is nonsense. Boilerplate terms can be worded in a variety of ways and these provisions can be as well drafted as the rest of the document.

These provisions are routine, but like real boilerplate making up a boiler in the hull of the ship or a local paper, they are very important. Without good boilerplate, the boiler explodes and the ship sinks, or the paper consists only of local interest stories and farm reports. To refer to these provisions as "housekeeping" provisions, as we do here, as when labeling anything "miscellaneous," tends to denigrate their importance. The term "boilerplate," when understood, reflects their fundamental importance as well as their routine nature.

8. Signature Blocks

Signature blocks provide a place for the parties and any witnesses to sign. If the party signing is an entity like a corporation, type the party's name above the signature line and identify the agent signing for the party by name and title below the signature line. If the party is an individual, type the name under the signature line. Signatures should not be on a page by themselves, so drafters include some of the text of the contract on the page on which the signatures appear. In addition, on extremely important documents, the parties should initial each page at the bottom.

Before the signature blocks, there is usually some introductory language, which some drafters call a testimonium clause. Like other standard provisions in agreements, this language can become ossified into archaic legalese. Contemporary drafters delete phrases such as "In Witness Whereof" and "as of the date that first appears above" and use a modern, plain English provision. For example:

The Parties agree to the terms of the Agreement, above.

—or—

To show that they have agreed to the terms of this agreement, the Parties have executed this Agreement below on [the date stated on page 1 or the date(s) indicated below].

—or—

Agreed.

To avoid inconsistent dating of documents, the introductory language to a signature block often refers to a date appearing on the first page or paragraph of the document. This is fine, as long as that date is filled in. Too many times, in the heat of closing, the parties simply flip to the last page of the agreement, which they have already reviewed many times before negotiations, and fail to note that the date on page 1 has been left blank. In another form that is common in practice, the agreement is dated "as of" a date contained on the first page (filled in early in the drafting process) and the signature blocks are undated or contain the date of execution by the parties.

Drafters use "as of" when the signing date differs from the agreement's effectiveness date, i.e., parties intend that an agreement signed on September 1st is effective "as of" September 10th.

Take care with party names and make sure you get them exactly right. Issues of punctuation are especially easy to miss, such as commas and periods, and descriptors of limited liability status, such as "LLC" or "Inc." For example, "Allen Bates & Lebowitz LLP" could be a limited liability partnership that is the successor to "Allen, Bates & Lebowitz" a general partnership and is legally distinct from the former entity, or a professional corporation. Many jurisdictions allow the formation of entities with very similar names, which might differ only by a comma or spelling out the word "and" rather than using an ampersand (&). Train your eye to notice details of this nature. It is embarrassing when the client catches the mistake at the closing. It is even worse when the error is not uncovered until it is the subject of later litigation.[4]

Here is a sample signature block:

To evidence the parties' agreement to this Agreement, they have signed it on the date stated in the preamble.

Apex Property, LLC

By: _Homer J. Simpson_
Homer J. Simpson
President

Because Apex Property, LLC is not a natural person, an officer or some other agent has to sign on its behalf. In the above example, Apex's president, Homer J. Simpson, signed. Note that the person signs on the "By" line and his position is written below his typed name. For an individual, you simply insert a line and type the individual's name under it. Make sure that the names in the signature blocks match the names specified in the contract's preamble.

C. Substantive Provisions in More Detail

Transactional attorneys use terms of art to describe different types of substantive provisions of an agreement discussed in §§ 5 and 6 above. These include definitions, representations and warranties, covenants, and conditions.

---

4   *See, e.g.,* Tryingham Holdings, Inc. 354 B.R. 363 (Bankr. E.D. Va. 2006).

1. Defined Terms

Using defined terms enhances clarity by specifying the meaning of a word or phrase used in a contract. Here's an example from a chicken purchase agreement:

> *1.* **Definitions.** *The following terms have the meanings assigned to them:*
>
> **"Chicken"** *means an eviscerated frozen young chicken suitable for broiling and frying.*

As explained above, defining a term saves the drafter having to repeat a wordy definition numerous times throughout the contract, which makes the contract easier to draft and read. Defining a term also reduces the risk of the drafter inadvertently referring to the same thing in a different way (for example, referring to "eviscerated frozen young chickens" in one place and "eviscerated frozen chickens" in another). Using different language to cover the same concept is a major mistake because it makes it unclear whether the parties intended different concepts, and thus could give rise to litigation.

To enhance readability, select as your defined term a word or a phrase that is informative and concise. For example, for "eviscerated frozen young chicken suitable for broiling and frying" use "Chicken" instead of "EFYC" (which is concise but uninformative) or "Eviscerated Young Chicken" (which is informative but not concise).

A contract can have a separate definition section as the above example demonstrates or define terms in context. Here is an example where the term "Chickens" is defined in context:

> *Seller shall sell to Buyer 500 eviscerated frozen young chickens suitable for broiling and frying (the **"Chickens"**).*

It is common for a contract to define some terms in context and some terms in a definition section.

When defining a term most attorneys give it initial capital letters and put it in quotes. Many drafters also bold or underline the term where it is defined to aid the reader in locating the definition. To signify that you are using a previously defined term in the contract, simply capitalize the word (do not put it in quotes, bold it, or underline it).

Don't get carried away with using defined terms. If a concept only appears once in a contract, there is no need to create a defined term for it. Further, it is unnecessary to define a term that has a well settled meaning (assuming you're using the term in its normal sense). For example, defining "Month" as "each of the twelve named periods into which a year is divided" is overkill. Just go with the undefined term "month."

2. Representations and Warranties

Representations and warranties, or "reps" for short, are assertions of fact by the contracting parties. They generally serve one of two purposes: (1) to ensure that a party either receives what the party is expecting to receive under the contract or has a breach of contract claim against the other party; and (2) to allocate the risk of an unknown fact to one of the parties. For example, when purchasing a used car, it is a good idea to include in the purchase agreement, among other things, a representation and warranty that the car's odometer reflects the actual number of miles the car has been driven. Here is an example:

> *Seller represents and warrants to Buyer as follows: The Car's odometer reads 33,340 miles, which is the actual number of miles the Car has been driven.*

If it turns out that the car's odometer has been rolled back, then Buyer did not get the car she expected (one with 33,340 miles on it). Buyer will have a breach of contract claim against Seller because the representation and warranty Seller made to Buyer is false. In other words, the representation and warranty has allocated the risk of the odometer being inaccurate to Seller by giving Buyer recourse against Seller if the odometer turns out to be inaccurate. Conversely, if the contract was silent on the car's odometer reading, Buyer implicitly assumes the risk of an inaccurate odometer. In that case, Buyer does not have any recourse against Seller under the contract because Seller did not represent and warranty to Buyer that the odometer reflected the actual miles driven.

Whether Seller agrees to include the above representation and warranty in the contract will likely be the subject of negotiations between the parties and may affect other parts of the contract. For example, the parties may initially agree on a sale of price of $12,000. However, when Buyer insists on getting an odometer representation and warranty from Seller, Seller may agree to provide it only if Buyer agrees to pay $12,250 for the car. Essentially, Buyer would pay Seller an additional $250 for Seller to assume the risk of an inaccurate odometer.

Alternatively, Seller could agree to provide the representation and warranty if it contains a knowledge qualifier. In such a case, the language would read "The Car's odometer reads 33,340 miles, which, to *Seller's knowledge*, is the actual number of miles the Car has been driven." Under the language, Buyer is protected if Seller knows the odometer ha been rolled back but has withheld this information from Buyer. However, Buyer is not protected if it turns out that the odometer has been rolled back but Seller had no knowledge of it. We will cover qualified representations and warranties in exercise #5.

3. Covenants

A covenant is simply a promise to do or not to do something. "Affirmative covenants" promise to do something, and "negative covenants" promise not to do something. Lawyers use covenants to identify the rights and duties of each party, including issues that may come up during the gap period between the date when the contract is signed and when the whole transaction is finalized or "closed."

For example, one reason the purchase of a home typically involves a delayed closing is because most buyers need to obtain financing in order to close. However, in this situation, a seller may be concerned that a buyer will drag her feet in obtaining financing or sour on the house and purposely not pursue financing. To address this issue, a lawyer could include a financing covenant in the contract. Here's an example:

> *Buyer shall use Buyer's best efforts to obtain a loan within thirty days of the date of this Agreement sufficient to enable Buyer to pay Seller the Purchase Price at Closing.*

Similarly, the buyer may be concerned that the seller will fail to properly maintain the property during the gap period. To address this issue, a lawyer could include the following covenant in the contract:

> *Seller shall maintain and, if necessary, repair the Premises so that at Closing all heating, cooling, mechanical, plumbing, and electrical systems and all built-in appliances are in working condition.*

Covenants do not guarantee that the party will do—or not do—what the party promised, but they do provide the other party with a breach of contract claim in the event the covenant is not met. In addition, a breached covenant can give the non-breaching party an option to not close. Lawyers call that provision a "condition."

4. Conditions

A condition is something that must be satisfied before some other legal consequence attaches. Express conditions are the mechanisms that control how a transaction progresses. Non-satisfaction of a condition simply means that the legal consequence does not come to pass. A condition thus differs from a duty, in that the party charged with satisfying a condition is not liable in damages for a failure to do so.

Conditions are often written in an "If . . . then . . ." format. For example:

> *If Buyer fails to pay for the Goods prior to delivery, then Seller may cancel its obligations under this Agreement, including its duty to deliver the Goods.*

There are several types of conditions. A condition may relate to the conduct of the parties. A seller, for example, may have no duty to ship the goods until the buyer has paid in full. Or a condition may relate to external events, which are referred to as "contingencies." Thus, a seller may have no duty to ship until an embargo ends.

Closing conditions specify conditions that must be fulfilled or waived before a party is obligated to close on the transaction. Here are some examples:

> *Conditions to Buyer's Obligations. Buyer's obligation to close the Sale is subject to the satisfaction of the following conditions:*
>
> *(A) <u>Representations and Warranties</u>: Seller's representations and warranties must be true on the Closing Date.*
>
> *(B) <u>Covenants</u>: Seller must have performed all of the covenants to be performed by it on or before the Closing Date.*

Notice that the above closing conditions are tied to representations, warranties, and covenants made by Seller elsewhere in the contract. Consequently, if a representation and warranty turns out to be false—even if it is true when the contract was signed—or Seller fails to comply with one of its covenants, Buyer would not have to close on the transaction.

Oftentimes a contract that contemplates a delayed closing also includes a provision that allows one or both parties to unilaterally terminate a contract if the closing conditions have not been fulfilled or waived by a specified date. Transactional attorneys call this date a "drop-dead date" and the condition a "walk-away condition."

Now you have the basic tools to read and discuss a contract using the terms of art employed by transactional lawyers.

D. Drafting Applied: Identifying Contract Components Within a Note

The template below is a standard fixed rate note. In the right margin identify the anatomical parts that make up a contract's skeleton and the contractual concepts that reflect the substance of the parties' agreement, all of which are indicated in blue. To review: Anatomical parts are title, preamble, recitals, words of agreement and consideration, headings, testimonium clause, and signature block. Contractual concepts are declarations, definitions, representations and warranties, covenants, conditions, endgame provisions, and boilerplate.

NOTE   _____

_____, _____ _____, _____

      [Date]   [City]   [State]

_____   _____

[Borrower name] ("Borrower") [Entity designation and property address]

Background

Lender, as defined below, and Borrower seek to memorialize Lender's loan of funds to Borrower   _____

ACCORDINGLY, the parties agree as follows: _____

1. BORROWER'S PROMISE TO PAY

In return for a loan that Borrower has received, Borrower   _____
promises to pay U.S. $_____ ("Principal"), plus
interest, to the order of _____
___ ("Lender"), a New York corporation located at _____
_____
_____.

Lender may transfer this Note.

---

2. INTEREST

Interest will be charged on unpaid principal until the full amount of Principal has been paid. Borrower will pay interest at a yearly rate of _____%.

The interest rate required by this Section 2 is the rate Borrower will pay both before and after any default described in Section 6(B) of this Note.

3. PAYMENTS

(A) Time and Place of Payments

Borrower shall pay principal and interest by making a payment on the _____ day of each month beginning on _____, _____ by sending a check or money order to Lender's address first noted above or at a different address if required.

Borrower shall make these payments every month until it has paid all of the principal and interest and any other charges described below that it owes under this Note. Lender will apply each monthly payment as of its scheduled due date and will apply payments to interest before Principal. If, on _____, 20____, ("Maturity Date") Borrower still owes amounts under this Note, it will pay those amounts in full on that date.

(B) Amount of Monthly Payments

Borrower's monthly payment will be in the amount of U.S. $_____ _____.

4. BORROWER'S RIGHT TO PREPAY

Borrower has the right to make payments of Principal at any   _____ time before they are due ("Prepayment"). When Borrower makes a Prepayment, Borrower will tell the Note Holder in writing that it is doing so. Borrower may not designate a payment as a Prepayment if Borrower has not made all the monthly payments due under the Note.

Borrower may make a full Prepayment or partial Prepayments without paying a Prepayment charge. Lender will use any Prepayments to reduce the amount of Principal that Borrower owes under this Note. However, Lender may apply any Prepayment to the accrued and unpaid interest on the Prepayment amount before applying that Prepayment to reduce the Principal amount of the Note. If Borrower makes a partial Prepayment, there will be no changes in the due date or in the amount of the monthly payment unless Lender agrees in writing to those changes.

5. LOAN CHARGES

If a law that applies to this loan and which sets maximum loan charges is finally interpreted so that the interest or other loan charges collected or to be collected in connection with this loan exceed the permitted limits, then Lender shall: (a) reduce any loan charge by the amount necessary to make the charge comply with the permitted limit; and (b) refund to Borrower any sums already collected that exceeded permitted limits. Lender may choose to make this refund by reducing the Principal owed under this Note or by making a direct payment to Borrower. If a refund reduces Principal, the reduction will be treated as a partial Prepayment.

6. PURPOSE OF NOTE

Borrower represents and warrants that the loan evidenced by this Note was made solely for the purpose of carrying on or acquiring a business or commercial enterprise.

7. BORROWER'S FAILURE TO PAY AS REQUIRED

(A) Late Charge for Overdue Payments

If Lender has not received the full amount of any monthly payment by the end of _____ calendar days after the date it is due, Borrower must pay a late charge to Lender. The amount of the charge will be 5% of that overdue payment of principal and interest. Borrower must pay this late charge promptly but only once on each late payment.

(B) Default

If Borrower does not pay the full amount of each monthly payment on the date it is due, Borrower will be in default ("Default").

(C) Notice of Default

If Borrower is in Default, Lender may send Borrower a written notice telling it that if it does not pay the overdue amount by a certain date, Lender may require Borrower to pay immediately the full amount of Principal which has not been paid and all the interest owed on that amount ("Acceleration"). That date must be at least 30 days after the date on which Lender mails the notice to Borrower or delivers it by other means.

(D) No Waiver

If at a time when Borrower is in default Lender does not Accelerate, Lender still has the right to do so if Borrower is in default at a later time.

(E) Payment of Lender's Costs and Expenses

If the Lender has Accelerated then Borrower must pay Lender for all costs and expenses Lender incurred in enforcing this Note to the extent not prohibited by applicable law. Those expenses include, for example, reasonable attorneys' fees.

8. GIVING OF NOTICES

Unless applicable law requires a different method, any notice that must be given under this Note must be given by delivering it or by mailing it by first class mail to either Borrower or Lender as applicable at the Property Address above or at a different address if either party gives the other a notice of a different address.

9. OBLIGATIONS OF PERSONS UNDER THIS NOTE

Any person who is a guarantor, surety or endorser of this Note is also obligated to do these things.

[space left intentionally blank]

10. WAIVERS

Borrower and any other person who has obligations under this Note waive the rights of Presentment and Notice of Dishonor.

The parties have executed and delivered this Note on the date first written above.

_____

Name of Borrower

By:_____   _____

Person signing for Borrower

Title of Borrower's agent

Part II: Negotiation Essentials

A. Types of Negotiation Explained

Now that you know the anatomical parts of a contract—title, preamble, words of agreement, etc.—and the contractual concepts like representations, warranties, and covenants that convey contractual rights and duties, you are ready to engage in the first step of a transactional lawyer's practice. To memorialize an agreement on paper—or the screen—an attorney must understand the business transaction at hand. Look at the Term Sheet set out in the Introduction. It tells you the names of the parties that you will use in the preamble, the interest rate, and other facts that you can fill in. (The reference to Bianca Bolt personally guarantying the loan is relevant only if you are assigned exercise #7 on the personal guaranty.)

Bianca Bolt and Lamar Lee are still negotiating the amount of the loan. They have agreed that the bank will loan the LLC $600,000, but Bianca would like to increase the loan amount to $800,000 to make improvements in the Store. The bank, for its part, might lend the higher amount if the higher risk were offset by another term of the note or security agreement.

B. Theory and Tips for Successful Negotiation.[5]

There are two primary types of bargaining. In *positional bargaining,* the parties view the negotiation as a zero-sum game where one party's gain is equivalent to the other party's loss. In *interest-based bargaining,* the parties view the negotiation as a problem-solving process rather than a zero-sum game. The parties are perceived to have complementary or mutual interests, so that bargain may result in overall gains for both sides.

In positional bargaining, each party typically starts the negotiation from an extreme negotiation position (high or low amount of the loan, for example). The party's expectation is that small concessions gradually will be made by each side until a moderate or middle ground outcome is reached. Bluffing and puffing is common as the parties negotiate. Be aware that when an attorney negotiates on behalf of a client, lying is prohibited as a violation of the lawyer's professional responsibilities under Rule 4.1 of the Model Rules of Professional Conduct.

Common strategies used in positional bargaining are:

1.   make the other side offer first;

2.   make the other side compromise first;

3.   claim a lack of authority to do what the other side requests;

4.   act irrationally; and

5.   claim that the other side is irrational or making unreasonable demands.

---

5   Excerpted from Colleen E. Medill, *Developing Professional Skills: Property* 47 (2012)

In interest-based bargaining, each party focuses on the problem to be solved and tries to identify at least one area of common interest where mutual gains may be achieved. Creative solutions are used to accommodate the goals and objectives of the parties.

Common strategies used in interest-based bargaining are:

1. focus on the problem, not the people or their personalities;

2. focus on the mutual interests of the parties, not on fixed demands or positions;

3. emphasize points of collaboration, not confrontation; and

4. empathize with the needs of the other side.

Depending on the circumstances, lawyers who are effective negotiators often use a combination of positional and interest-based bargaining to achieve the best result for their clients.

Negotiation Lines and Phrases

If you enjoy playing poker, you are likely to enjoy negotiating. Imagine that you represent Bolt's Urban Hardware or its landlord as they negotiate the terms of the lease on the premises where the Store is located. Review the following list of negotiation lines and phrases that the landlord or tenant could use to negotiate the rent.

Tenant Urban Hardware

- The rent you are demanding is for a property that is perfect. This property is not perfect. [Describe deficiencies or defects in the property.]

- Your allowance for interior finish is inadequate. If my client has to supplement the allowance, then we want a corresponding reduction in the rent.

- If my client is contributing to the cost of the interior finish, then my client wants to pick the contractor to do the work.

- The [insert characteristic, e.g., parking, loading dock, etc.] for this property is inadequate when compared with similar properties for rent in this market. That calls for a rent reduction.

- There is a surplus of vacant retail space in the market right now. Can't you be more reasonable?

- Other landlords would love to work with my client. Why can't you be more accommodating?

- Is your client prejudiced against my client because my client is [insert client characteristic]?

Landlord

- This is quality new construction with a generous allowance for standard interior finish. My client has to cover the costs and expenses of construction and still meet payroll.

- If my client has to pay extra for the interior finish, then the rent will go up.

- My client needs to select the contractor to ensure quality control over the work product.

- Vacancy rates are higher for older buildings; this is new construction.

- Lots of tenants would love the deal I am offering.

- My client has been in the business of owning and operating real estate for over ___ years. This is a reasonable offer.

- It is not reasonable for your tenant to demand that my client must pour more money into this asset.

- Can you really afford to lease this property?

Generic (Anyone, any type of negotiation)

- Do you really think that is a potential problem? Why are you so worried about something that is so unlikely to happen?

- My client will never agree to that term.

- I'll try to reason with my client, but you shouldn't expect too much.

- No one can predict the future. My client needs flexibility.

- I understand your client needs flexibility. But my client needs flexibility, too.

- Your client would have to agree and sign off on that provision.

- I can't advise my client to sign that.

- Everyone has to give up something to make this deal happen.

- Is that your best offer?

- I've talked with my client, and this is my best offer.

- My client is honest and has integrity. My client would never do such a bad thing.

- This is how everyone else in town does it.

- We need to address this issue expressly in the lease. I don't want to end up litigating over it

C. Application: Negotiation Assignment

Your professor may provide additional instructions to each side of the transaction that set out what the clients have told their attorneys. If so, remember that professional ethics require you to keep confidential your communications with your client, so read only your own client's instructions and do not disclose your client's confidences to your negotiating partner.

Negotiation is more likely to be successful if you justify a proposal that you make with a reason that shows that it is in the other person's interest to include the term or that it increases the chance of a successful transaction. Before you start negotiating with your partner, take a few minutes to make a list of what your client wants and identify one or two reasons that some or all of the terms can be good for both parties. Consider what your client is willing to give up in order to get that good term (i.e., the debtor could provide additional collateral to get a loan for more money). Then sit down with your negotiation partner and determine the amount of the loan and any additional provisions such as terms that the bank requires in exchange for lending the Store more than $600,000.

Part III: Legal Rules: Negotiable Instruments Under UCC Article 3

As you draft, keep two legal doctrines in mind. First, UCC §9–203 requires that the creditor gives "value" for a security interest to attach to collateral. While UCC §1–204 defines "value" broadly to include even partial satisfaction of a pre-existing claim, secured transactions commonly involve a new loan evidenced by a promissory note.

Second, most lenders want a note to be "negotiable." Payments courses explore the precise requirements of negotiability, the precondition for a panoply of lender rights under UCC Article 3. For present purposes, we need only note that UCC §§3–103 and 3–104 define "negotiable instrument" as "an unconditional promise . . . to pay a fixed amount of money" that must be written and signed by the person "undertaking to pay" and has certain magic words making it negotiable. [6]

Together these provisions illustrate a larger point that many law students miss. Some contract terms are much more important than others. If a creditor does not give "value" or if a debtor does not sign the promissory note, you have failed to create a binding contract. All you have is a worthless piece of paper instead of a right to collect thousands or even millions of dollars. You job may well be on the line and your malpractice insurance carrier will probably get involved.

---

[6] Negotiability is a commercial law concept that makes written promise to pay money freely transferable, and thus akin to money.

Part IV: Student Assignment: Memorialize the Deal

Having completed the first three steps—learning the components of a contract, negotiation basics, and reviewing the relevant legal rules— you are ready to reduce your agreement to a writing (or "record" in the terminology of the UCC if you pass in your work electronically).[7] You have determined the loan terms and know the format in which trans- actional lawyers memorialize those terms. Go to the book website and download the sample promissory note, which is the same as the one featured in Part I of this exercise. Fill in the blanks to make the note fit the transaction between the Bolt's Urban Hardware and FNB.

A. Drafting Tips

- Draft the preamble and signature blocks at the same time to ensure that you have the names of the parties correct.

- Be sure to properly identify the agency of Bianca Bolt and Lamar Lee in signature blocks.

- Conform the note template to the terms you negotiate with your partner regarding the amount of loan and the day of the month on which each payment is due. If your professor assigns multiple exercises over the course of the semester, you could date them all on the last date of class so that the portfolio of documents all bear the same date.

- You can calculate the monthly payments for a 10-year loan of that amount at 5% interest on a website such as bankrate.com (http://www.bankrate.com/calculators/ managing-debt/loan-calculator.aspx).

---

7   UCC § 1–201(b)(31) defines "record" as "information that is transcribed in a tangible medium or that is stored in an electronic or other medium and is retrievable in perceivable form."

- Make sure to delete elements of the form that are no longer necessary once you fill in the details from this transaction, such as bracketed references to dates or the blank lines that indicate where that information should be inserted.

- Be sure to include the debtor's signature—without it a promissory note is not legally binding. You can "sign" for your client's agent by inserting his or her name on the signature line in a font that looks like handwriting.

B. Checklist for a Contract's Essential Parts

❏ Title

❏ Preamble

❏ Recitals

❏ Words of agreement and statement of consideration

❏ Definitions
  - i.e., Parties

❏ Action Sections
  - Amount of debt
  - Interest rate
  - Dates when payments due

❏ Other Substantive Provisions
  - Days before late penalty assessed

❏ Endgame
  - Default

❏ General provisions (boilerplate)

❏ Signature Block
- Names correct
- Agency correctly stated

Front Matter and Signature Blocks

Skill: Contract Formatting

Overview

THIS EXERCISE focuses on drafting the skeleton of a contract: introductory provisions that are often called "front matter" as well as the testimonium clause and signature blocks. Together the front matter, testimonium clause and signature blocks operate as bookends that contain the substantive contract provisions. Contracts begin with the title, preamble, recitals, and words of agreement and consideration, and end with a testimonium clause and signature blocks.

As with exercise #1, you will edit a template. Here, the precedent agreement is a security agreement, one which was used to memorialize a similar transaction to FNB's financing of the hardware store acquisition. Working with the template promissory note in exercise #1 and the template security agreement in this and the coming exercises gives you hands-on experience with how different types of contracts reflect the governing legal doctrine as well as conventions for each type of agreement.

Practicing lawyers generally revise templates over time. They learn that a particular phrase caused confusion in another transaction, so they update a form contract to reflect evolving legal rules. New lawyers develop a sense over time of why and how they are using a particular template and every term included in that template. As you look at this template and others that you come across, remember that just because a provision was in the last deal that used this template does not mean that it must also be relevant to the current deal.

Over time a lawyer develops his own style of writing agreements and wants to present a well-written document to the client. Yet the timeline for a particular transaction often precludes detailed wordsmithing such as transforming passive voice to active voice in the whole document. Most clients are unwilling to pay their lawyer to perfect a template that will benefit the lawyer's future clients. (Moreover, as we will explore in exercise #9 on legal ethics in drafting, billing a client for that extra work may pose ethical dangers.) Accordingly, you will edit discrete parts of the security agreement over the course of exercises #2, #4, #5 and #6, just as a lawyer might over a series of transactions.

Starting with this exercise, you will make stylistic decisions based on the material on legal drafting below, and use them consistently throughout this exercise and the ones that come later. Exercise #4 has you revise the core business provisions of the contract to make a security interest attach to the collateral. Exercise #5 requires you to delve deeper into the transaction's details to write and edit other substantive provisions such as the debtor's representations about its good standing as an LLC, its covenants not to transfer the collateral, and declarations by both parties regarding how to give each other notice. The last security agreement exercise focuses on the last substantive provisions of the contract, which logically appear at the end of the document itself. In exercise #6, students negotiate and draft endgame provisions about default and foreclosure on the collateral.

In this exercise Part I begins by explaining the central tasks in drafting: achieving precision, clarity, and consistency. It then discuses how lawyers review contracts. Part II applies these lessons by having you draft a contract's front and end matter.

Part I: Drafting Essentials Explained

Students are often surprised to learn that there is more than one style of writing contracts. The two main forms are known as "traditional" and either "contemporary" or "plain English." Traditional legal writing looks like what most lay people think of as a "real" contract, with lots of "whereases," "hereafters," and fancy phrases like "by and between" and "know all men by these presents." Some lawyers still draft that way. But increasingly business people and transactional lawyers prefer contemporary drafting. Contemporary drafting yields a document that is clearer and more concise so that a reader gets to the point before her eyes glaze over. It can also help a drafter achieve the crucial task of avoiding errors and ambiguity. Wordiness may look impressive, but it can cover up the meaning the parties intend and even create ambiguity.

A. Precision, Clarity and Consistency

Much of the template you will use in this and subsequent exercises is written in the traditional style that you should update to contemporary drafting. The material below also explains other aspects of good drafting: correctly identifying the agreement's subject matter, date, and parties, often by defining terms and avoiding legalese. Finally, this chapter describes the way that lawyers and business people review a document. It illustrates common editorial marks that attorneys often use to tell a junior attorney, colleague, client or opposing counsel how to alter a document, which your professor may also use in grading your work.

Like any new and complex task, learning to critically read a contract and write one well takes time and practice. This exercise helps you spot problematic writing and how to correct it.

1. Avoid Ambiguity[1]

The primary goal of a contract is to set forth the terms of the contracting parties' agreement in language that subsequent readers
will interpret in exactly the same way. This goal is achieved through
precise drafting. A precise contract is one that is free from ambiguity.
Ambiguity is present when each party can attach different meanings to
a contractual provision.

For example, you may have read the case *Frigaliment Importing Co. v.
B.N.S. International Sales Corp.*, 190 F. Supp. 116 (S.D.N.Y. 1960) for your
Contracts class. In that case, Frigaliment entered into two contracts
with B.N.S. for the purchase of frozen chickens. Frigaliment thought
the term chicken mean a "broiler" (a young chicken suitable for broiling
and frying). Conversely, B.N.S. thought it meant any bird of the chicken
genus. Thus B.N.S. shipped Frigaliment stewing chickens. Because
stewing chickens are inferior to broilers, Frigaliment sued B.N.S. for
breach of contract. As the court recognized, "the word 'chicken' standing
alone is ambiguous." It could mean a broiler or it could mean a stewing
chicken, but the contract did not specify. Hence, the dispute may have
been avoided had the contract drafter simply included a more precise
description of what B.N.S. was to ship, saving the parties the time and
expense of litigation and preserving an amicable business relationship.

Learning to draft with precision is a skill developed over time by
working with contracts. Let's assume you are assigned the task of
drafting a contract for the sale of frozen chicken but have never read or
heard about *Frigaliment*. Hence, you make the same mistake that was
made in that case and use the term "chicken" instead of more precise
terminology like "a young chicken suitable for broiling and frying."
There is a good chance that someone else involved with the deal
(e.g. a supervising attorney, the attorney for the other side, the client)
will flag "chicken" as ambiguous (maybe because the person has read

---

1   Based on William K. Sjostrom, Jr., *An Introduction to Contract Drafting* 35–40 (2d ed. 2013).

Frigaliment or has worked on chicken deals in the past). You will then know that "chicken" is ambiguous and use more precise terminology in your contract and all future chicken contracts you draft. In addition, you will also, hopefully, keep the ambiguity of "chicken" in mind when drafting contracts for turkey, duck, and pig deals, which will lead you to ask the client whether the contract should use more precise terminology than just "turkey," or "duck," or "pig." Over time, you will be clued in to more and more potentially ambiguous contractual language and will therefore get better and better at stripping it out of the contracts you draft and review.

A clearly drafted contract is easy to read. Clarity is important because if a contract is confusing to read, the parties may be unable to decipher what exactly it says and therefore not realize until after it is signed that the contract does not reflect the intended deal. Contract clarity is achieved through some of the same techniques employed by various types of writers. These techniques include short sentences, active voice, logical organization, consistency, and descriptive headers. Future exercises explore those topics. We start here with practices that impact clarity and are unique to drafting contracts.

2. Precisely State Dates

Drafters take equal care with a seemingly simple matter, the date of the agreement. They state the date only once in an agreement—usually in the the preamble—to avoid a situation such as the document being dated June 6 in the preamble and June 16 in the testimonium clause.

Drafters also choose between two formats: either "June 6, 2017," or "as of June 6, 2017." The first format makes the document binding on the day that it is signed, which should happen on June 6. 2017. Beware of the seemingly dignified phrase "as of." This second way to designate a date allows the parties to sign a document on one date and have it become effective on another date. For example, a preamble dating a contract "as of June 6, 2017," makes it binding as of that date, not when it's actually signed. Policing these details avoids arguments about when the parties became bound.

3. Trim Legalese

Legalese is arcane and often formalistic jargon used by lawyers in contracts. Here are some contractual provisions loaded up with legalese:

AGREEMENT FOR THE CONVEYANCE OF REAL ESTATE

THIS AGREEMENT FOR THE CONVEYANCE OF REAL ESTATE is entered into this 6th day of December, 2017, by, between, and among Robert C. Smith, an individual residing at 657 Water Street, Evanston, Illinois 60209 and Jane H. Borg, an individual residing at 7 Oak Divc, Northbrook, Illinois 60601.

WITNESSETH:

WHEREAS, the party of the first part is desirous of acquiring the party of the second part's abode;

WHEREAS, the party of the second part is amendable to selling the aforementioned abode pursuant to, and in accordance with, the terms as hereinafter provided;

NOW, THEREFORE, in consideration of the sum of One Dollar ($1.00) and other good and valuable consideration, the receipt and sufficiency of the same of which is hereby acknowledged, the party of the first part and the party of the second part herewith covenant and agree as hereinafter set forth:

* * *

IN WITNESS WHEREOF the parties hereto have hereunto set their hands and seals the day and year first above written.

That title, preamble, recitals, words of agreement, and concluding or testimonium clause could and should be written without the "whereas," "hereinafter," "hereby," and other flowery language, along the following lines:

HOUSE SALE AGREEMENT

*This House Sale Agreement (**"Agreement"**), dated December 6, 2017, is between Robert C. Smith, an individual residing at 657 Water Street, Evanston, Illinois 60209 (**"Buyer"**) and Jane H. Borg, an individual residing at 7 Oak Drive, Northbrook, Illinois 60601 (**"Seller"**).*

• Skill: Contract Formatting

> ### *Background*
>
> *This agreement provides for the sale of a home by Seller to Buyer.*
>
> *Accordingly, the parties agree as follows:*
>
> ** * **
>
> *To evidence the parties' agreement to this Agreement, they have signed it on the date stated in the preamble.*

The rewritten version does not change the substance of the agreement but is much easier to read than the original version. Stripping out the legalese achieved this improved clarity, which you can do when drafting and reviewing contracts.[2]

Legalese often occurs in phrases of two or three words, commonly known as doublets or triplets. These famous repetitious chains of words are part of the hoary legal chant that has come down through the ages. Examples include: "null and void;" "settlement and compromise;" "swear and affirm;" "right, title and interest;" and others listed below.

Ask: Do I really need each of these terms? Will fewer do? Will listing these terms leave the provision vulnerable to the doctrine of *expressio unis et exclusio alterius*?[3] It may be tempting to think that a proper interpretive doctrine or equitable maxim will assist in correcting any

---

2   Use your judgment when applying this rule. For example, you may not want to cross out or rewrite all unnecessary legalese when reviewing a contract as doing so may irritate the other party's attorney, making it more difficult to work with the person on the transaction, or be viewed by your client or the other side as "over-lawyering." Because the same concerns are not present when you are doing the initial draft, you should normally strip out all legalese. However, if a senior attorney gives you a sample to start with that she characterizes as "good" or something similar, you may want to refrain from doing a major rewrite out of political concerns.

3   A rule of contract interpretation that means that saying one thing implicitly excludes another. We will address the dangers of *expressio unis* in exercise #3's description of collateral.

ambiguity in documents that you draft. The problem is that for every doctrine or maxim that would favor one interpretation, there is another that will defeat it. These principles are largely ceremonial support for reaching the result that the court has determined is just rather than the reasoning that leads to that determination. If *expressio unis* may be a problem, consider using a more general term that contains within its meaning all desired alternatives.

At one time in English legal history, Norman French, Middle English, and Latin all competed to become the dominant or authoritative language of the law. The same legal concept could be expressed in three different languages. Cautious lawyers used the words from all three languages to ensure that they achieved the desired legal consequence. Even after the words evolved into English as we know it today, lawyers continued to use these chains—as if they were some religious talisman that would guard them against a claim of malpractice. Perhaps billing practices also contributed, since early document drafters, called "scriveners," were paid by the word.

The common couplet and triplet phrases are usually unnecessary. The drafter should generally pick the simplest word of the group and drop the others even though the alliterative quality of many phrases—"any and all" or "mend, maintain, and repair"—flows from the tongue and pen. A partial list of these traditional phrases[4] is as follows:

agree and covenant	any and all
all and every	assign, transfer, and set over
alter or change	assumes and agrees
annul and set aside	attorney and counselor at law

4   List of couplets and triplets based on Haggard and Kuney, *Legal Drafting* 243–245 (2d ed. 2007).

authorize, direct, and empower

business, enterprise, or undertaking

by and with

cancel, annul, and set aside

cease and desist

changes, variations, and modifications

confessed and acknowledged

contract, agreement, covenant, and understanding

convey, transfer, and set over

costs, charges, and expenses

covenant and agree

deem and consider

do, execute, and perform

due and owing

due and payable

each and all

each and every

entirely and completely

evidencing or relating to

excess and unnecessary

fair and equitable

fair and reasonable

final and conclusive

finish and complete

for and in consideration of

for and on behalf of

force and effect

free and clear

free and unfettered

from and after

full and complete

full force and effect

furnish and supply

give and grant

goods, chattels, and effects

good and sufficient

have, hold, and possess

if and when

in and for

in truth and in fact

indebtedness and liabilities

initiate, institute, or commence

kind and character

kind and nature

known and described as

legal, valid, and binding

lien, charge, or encumbrance

loans and advances

loss or damages

made and entered into

made and provided

maintenance and upkeep

mend, maintain, and repair

mentioned or referred to

modified and changed

nature or description

null, avoid, and if no force and effect

obligation and liability

obey, observe, and comply with

of and concerning

ordain and establish

order and direct

over, above, and in addition to

part and parcel

pay, satisfy, and discharge

perform and discharge

performance or observance

place, install, or affix

possession, custody, and control

power and authority

release and discharge

relieve and discharge

remise, release, and quitclaim

representations, understandings, and agreements

revoked and annulled

right, title, and interest

rights and remedies

save and except

sell, transfer, alienate, and dispose of

shun and avoid

signed, published, and declared

situate, lying, and being in

sole and exclusive

stipulate and agree

suffer or permit

suit, claim, or demand

supersede and displace

terminate, cancel, or revoke

then and in that event

true and correct

type and kind

understood and agreed

unless and until

vacate, surrender, and deliver possession void and of no effect

void and of no force

void and no value

When you spot legalese—which you will notice more and more of over this course—try to update it. The following list gives a sample of substitutions, though of course the proper fix depends on the provision's purpose:

Assumes and agrees → agrees

Deem and consider → deem

Fair and equitable → either "fair" or "equitable"

Good and sufficient → sufficient

Assign, transfer, and set over → transfer

By and with → either "by" or "with"

Do, execute and perform → either "do" or "perform"

Each and every → either "each" or "every"

For and on behalf of → for

Free and unfettered → either "free" or "unfettered"

Full force and effect → effective

Give and grant → grant

Kind and nature → kind

Legal, valid, and binding → legally binding

Made and provided → either "made" or "provided"

Modified and changed → modified

Obligation and liability → obligation

Power and authority → authority

Representations, understandings and agreements → representations

Kind and character → kind

Null, void, and of no force and effect → void

Sole and exclusive → exclusive

Suffer or permit → permit

As you update a template's legalese to state provisions in plain English, be aware that some courts interpret seeming synonyms as separate concepts. For example, a testimonium clause should state that the agreement is "executed and delivered" because some courts have interpreted "execute" as not including delivery of the document to the other party.

Problem 2.1: Fixing Legalese

Transform these common legalese phrases into plain English.

a. This 12th day of June, 2017

b. By and between

c. Cease and desist

d. Promises, covenants, and agreements

e. Free and clear

f. The parties hereto

g. Town Bank (hereinafter "Bank")

4. Consistently Use Defined Terms[5]

Definitions tell the reader what a particular word or phrase means. Well drafted definitions promote clarity, brevity, and consistency. As we saw in exercise #1, definitions:

- define terms and concepts that have previously established lexical (dictionary) meaning essentially creating a proper noun;

- resolve an ambiguity if terms have more than one possible meaning;

- clarify terms that have a vague lexical meaning; and

- add to or subtract from a lexical meaning.

Definitions are strong medicine, and drafters should use them sparingly and with care. A badly drafted definition will infect every portion of the document where the term is used. Keep the following considerations in mind as you create definitions:

- Overly broad or narrow definitions can inadvertently introduce ambiguity or reallocate benefits and burdens. Defined terms can also be used to intentionally cloud meaning.

- If you define a term, only use it in the defined sense in the document. If not, ambiguity crops up. While English composition classes often encourage the use of different words for the same concept to avoid repetitive prose, the rule is different in legal drafting. Use the same words for the same meanings every time.

---

5   Definition section based on Haggard and Kuney, *Legal Drafting: Process, Techniques and Exercises*, 282–289 (2d ed. 2007).

- To protect against inadvertent use of defined terms that may create ambiguity, many drafters adopt a standard form of defined term. Examples include: Initial Caps, ALL CAPS, *italics*, **boldface**, or underlining. The predominant form appears to be Initial Caps. The first time you use the term—when you define it—also put the term in bold font.

Initial capitalization drapes the defined term in the mantle of a proper noun. This is appropriate because, within the document, the term essentially becomes a proper noun. This book places the defined term in parentheses and quotes when it is initially defined, e.g.:

> ... *June 7, 2017* (**"Due Date"**).

When the defined term is later used, it is in initial capitals, but without quotes or bold font, e.g.:

> ... *on the Due Date, the Payer shall...*

This is not a perfect solution, as it really changes the problem from using the defined term in its defined sense every time to ensuring that defined terms are initial capped every time they are used. It is, however, the dominant solution in practice.

Finally, take care to make the definition either inclusive or exclusive. Consider, for example, whether trade secrets constitute Intellectual Property under each of the following definitions:

> Inclusive: *"Intellectual Property" means intellectual property as that term is generally used and includes all patents, copyrights, and trademarks.*
>
> Exclusive: *"Intellectual Property" means patents, copyrights, and trademarks.*
>
> Ambiguous: *"Intellectual Property" means and includes patents, copyrights, and trademarks.*

This assignment requires you to define the parties. The term sheet in the Introduction gives their names and states that the debtor is known by its trade name as well as the name listed in the Articles of Organization that brought the debtor into being.

Party definitions can be tricky. For example, if "Big Financial Co." is defined in a mutual settlement and release agreement to be "Big Financial Co., Inc.," and also all of its subsidiaries, parent corporation, officers, directors, employees, attorneys, and accountants, to give Big Financial Co.–related individuals the benefit of the release of all claims by the other side, then does the person signing have the authority to bind all those people and entities to claims they are giving up against the other side?

5. Clearly Designate Entities and Authority

Consistency makes a document read smoothly and inspires confidence that it states material correctly. If you define FNB as "the 'Lender'," then put "the" in front of "Lender" and any other parties throughout the document (i.e., "The Borrower has applied to the Lender"). If you prefer to designate the parties' roles without "the," then refer to them as if the defined term were a proper name. So, if you define FNB as "Lender," then the recital should read "Borrower has applied to Lender."

Remember that the parties here are artificial persons, one an LLC and the other a banking corporation. They need natural persons to sign for them, and those natural persons (Bianca Bolt and Lamar Lee) must have authority to bind the debtor or bank. Be sure that the signature block properly indicates that Bianca and Lamar are signing in their representative capacity, and that their titles accurately reflect the information in the term sheet in the Introduction.

Problem 2.2: Draft Preamble and Signature Block

Draft the preamble and signature block for this promissory note.

Bonnie Blumenthal is the managing member and owner of Bonnie's Beautiful Blooms. Bonnie's Beautiful Blooms is a limited liability company located in California that is borrowing money from First Bank, a California corporation. The agent signing for First Bank is Kevin Wong, whose title is Vice President of Commercial Lending. Bonnie's Beautiful Blooms is located at 123 Flower Power Lane, Weed, CA 96094. First Bank is located at 987 Corporate Way Boulevard, Edgewood CA 96094. The note is dated September 30, 2017.

B. Reviewing a Contract

Many attorneys markup draft contracts electronically, providing comments in "track changes" mode and comment bubbles in the margins of a document. However, many attorneys still markup hard copies to provide comments, especially when training a new associate. Here is a list of common proofreading marks that a supervising attorney or your professor is likely to employ to succinctly comment on and correct your draft documents:

Proofreader's Marks[6]

Mark	Example	Symbol
Bold	SUMMARY OF ARGUMENT	*b.f.*
Italic	N.Y. Times v. Sullivan	*ital*
Roman or lightface	*rom.* You can't be **serious.**	*l.f.*
Capital	in the 101st congress	*caps*
Lowercase	my Constitutional rights	*l.c.*
Small caps	Fed. R. Civ. P. 11.	*s.c.*
Flush left	1.5 The Parties.	
Center	Procedural History	
Full justify	is whether the word or phrase is	
Flush right	Page 9	
Insert space	submitted toarbitration	#
Delete	standard of of care	
Close up	meet ing of the minds	
Delete and close up	interdependent contractor	
Replace	collateral estoppel	e
Insert	ipsa res loquitr	u
Move	the assumption of risk	
New paragraph	event. If the burden or	¶
No paragraph	event. If the burden or	no ¶
Transpose	reasonable supsicion	*tr.*
Insert period or colon	real property He said "I never	
Insert semicolon or comma	Friday meanwhile nothing was	
Insert apostrophe	to present the States case	
Insert quotation marks	He said, Why me?	
Insert parentheses	four factors: 1 Who drafted the	
Insert hyphen	the phrasal adjective rule	
Insert en dash	the Taft Hartley Act	
Insert em dash	in a word freedom.	
Spell out	a bare majority of 6 justices	*spell out*
Use numerals	out of eighty-two lawyers asked	*numerals*
Ignore correction	to correct any clerical error	*stet*

6   Bryan A. Garner, *The Redbook: A Manual of Legal Style* (2013).

C. Tips for Clear Writing

Having explained about the characteristics of poor legal writing—ambiguity, inconsistency, and incomprehensibility—it is time to apply that information by writing well. Four tips for good writing proposed by the novelist and essayist George Orwell apply to all kinds of writing:

- Never use a long word where a short one will do;

- If it is possible to cut a word out, always cut it out;

- Never use the passive where you can use the active; and

- Never use a foreign phrase, a scientific word, or a jargon word if you can think of an everyday English equivalent; and

- Break any of these rules sooner than say anything outright barbarous.

That last rule about barbarism stems from Orwell's life-long campaign against totalitarianism, but provides an excellent reminder of how writing techniques can serve nefarious ends in contracts as well as politics.[7] Authoritarian regimes use incomprehensive writing to cover up their wrongdoings with statements such as "meetings were held; decisions were made" which allows the speaker to cover up who held the meetings, who decided, and what those decisions were. Similarly, poor drafting can obscure the parties' intent in a business transaction. Your job as a lawyer is to clearly state the parties' rights and duties so that they—and if necessary courts—can quickly and easily settle most disputes.

---

7   George Orwell, *Politics and the English Language* (1946; 2006).

Tip 1: Shoot for Short and Sweet

Orwell expressed his writing advice in the negative—avoiding bad writing—but it can be easier to follow positive prescriptions. Seven characteristics define the contemporary style of drafting, which some attorneys call Plain English. Follow these rules and you are well on your way to clear drafting of contracts and other documents such as letters, memos, briefs and pleadings.[8]

- Short sentences

- Definite, concrete, everyday language

- The active voice

- Tabular presentation of complex or multi-factor information

- Separate paragraphs and sections, with headings for separate concepts

- The absence of highly legal jargon, highly technical business terminology, and use of Latin or other foreign terms

- The absence of double or multiple negatives.

To shorten a sentence, use verbs instead of nouns, writing "notify" instead of "give notice to." So "Buyer shall notify Seller" is shorter and clearer than "Buyer shall give notice to Seller." Likewise, use possessives, writing "Buyer's business" instead of "the business of the Buyer."

The active voice better performs the essential task of a contract by articulating who must do what. To root out passive voice, review your

---

[8] Characteristics of plain English based on George Kuney, *The Elements of Contract Drafting* 19 (4th ed. 2014).

document for the verb "to be," which often appears in passive voice clauses such as "payments will be applied." Instead, the clause should read, "Lender shall apply payments." In addition to risking ambiguity—a fatal flaw of contract drafting—passive voice also impedes readability by forcing the reader to work harder to understand the provision.

Tip 2: Weed Out Legalese

Avoid legal doublets and triplets and replace legalese with plain English terms where possible. For example, replace "aforesaid" with "previous" or "prior." Replace "any and all" with "any." Change "by and between" to "between," and change "such Agreement" to "the Agreement." Delete "whereas" or replace it with "accordingly," as the context dictates.

As you edit the template smoke out long sentences, the passive voice, and legalese and convert them to short sentences written in the active voice with minimal jargon. You will find that your writing improves in other contexts, a skill that employers, clients and professors will appreciate.

Part II: Student Assignment: Drafting Front Matter & End Matter

A. Edit the Template to Match the Transaction

Edit the front matter, testimonium, and signature blocks of the security agreement below. The front matter includes: a title; a preamble restating the name of the agreement, identifying the parties and the date; recitals briefly explaining why Bolt's Urban Hardware and the Bank are entering the security agreement; and words of agreement that indicate the parties' assent to all of the terms that come afterwards.

Because this exercise involves only the front matter, testimonium clause and signature blocks, the template deletes substantive contract provisions that are not part of this assignment, leaving only the headers surrounded by brackets (i.e., "[creation of security interest])."

Download the template from the book site and edit it to make the document reflect the transaction between Bolt's Urban Hardware and FNB. Use the track changes function of your word processing system then create a separate document that incorporates the changes without showing the edits. Pass in the clean copy and retain the copy with tracked changes for your records.

B. Tips for the Exercise

- Shorten sentences, make passive voice active, and edit out legalese where possible.

- Consider whether it is necessary to include the template's reference to the signature being "under seal."

- Be consistent throughout the document (i.e., make sure to state the parties' names in precisely the same way in the preamble and signature block).

C. Checklist for Front Matter and Signature Blocks

Title

❑ Not too general or too specific

❑ Not too long

❏ Initial caps of key words or all caps

❏ Centered; boldface

Preamble

❏ Define parties by role or name

❏ Place nicknames after all identifying information of the party

❏ Correct, full names of parties

❏ State of incorporation and principal place of business (for company); residential address for individual

❏ If address included for one party, then address included for other party

Background/Recitals

❏ Puts agreement in context but does not say too much

❏ No covenants or other substantive provisions

Words of Agreement and Statement of Consideration

❏ No archaic language

❏ Short and sweet—"Accordingly, the parties agree as follows:"

❏ Appears at the end of the Background section; not set apart in separate section

Testimonium

❏ Plain English—no archaic language

❏ Contains prefatory language ("To evidence their agreement to the terms..." or "AGREED:")

Signature Blocks

❏ Correct, full names of parties

❏ Formatted properly (block flushed to right margin)

D. Template: Security Agreement

LOAN AND SECURITY AGREEMENT

THIS LOAN AND SECURITY AGREEMENT (this "Agreement") is made this 12th day of June, 2017, by and between SECOND BANK OF SPRINGFIELD (the "Lender"), with a mailing address for the purposes of this Agreement at 123 Fake St., Springfield, NY 13333, Attn: Milhause Van Houten, and GLOBAL PAINT & HARDWARE, Inc. (d/b/a Global Club Hardware), a New York corporation (the "Borrower"), with a chief executive office and mailing address for the purposes of this Agreement of 747 Hammer Dr., Shelbyville, NY 13332.

RECITALS

A. The Borrower is engaged in the business of operating a Club Hardware store (the "Business") at the following location: 747 Hammer Dr., Shelbyville, NY 13332 (the "Business Premises").

B. The Borrower has applied to the Lender for a term loan in the original principal amount of $350,000 (the "Term Loan," and all other extensions of credit by the Lender to the Borrower being sometimes hereinafter referred to collectively as the "Loans").

C. The Lender is willing to provide the Loans on the condition that the Borrower enters into this Agreement, which shall, among other things, govern and secure the Loans.

NOW, THEREFORE, in consideration of the foregoing and of the mutual promises, covenants and agreements of the parties contained in this Agreement, the parties do agree as follows:

[Interpretation.]

[The Loans.]

[Creation of Security Interest.]

[Borrower Representations and Warranties regarding authority, etc.]

[Borrower Covenants regarding reporting, etc.]

[Default.]

[Remedies.]

[Space left intentionally blank.]

[Other Agreements.]

IN WITNESS WHEREOF, the parties hereto have caused this Agreement to be executed under seal and delivered as of the day and year first above written.

GLOBAL PAINT & HARDWARE, Inc.
d/b/a Global Club Hardware

By: _____

Patricia Bouvier
President

SECOND BANK OF SPRINGFIELD

By: _____

Milhause Van Houten
Senior Vice President

Financing Statement

Skill: Due Diligence

Overview

THIS EXERCISE PROVIDES essential information and practice in due diligence, contract review, and searching the UCC files to determine a creditor's priority. Because most creditors file a financing statement before finalizing the security agreement you too will fill out a financing statement before drafting the security agreement.

Getting the debtor's name precisely right on the financing statement is essential. Misspellings and other errors can render a financing statement ineffective and thus deprive a secured party of its perfected security interest. That error can mean losing out to the bankruptcy trustee or other creditors.

Accordingly, the contract drafting materials in Part I of this exercise include information about how a lawyer's professional standing turns on her attention to detail, tips to prevent errors, and basics about the contract drafting process. Part II recaps the legal rules that determine a financing statement's effectiveness and has you apply this information with a hands-on search in New York's UCC-1 files to see if competing creditors could have priority over FNB. In Part III, you negotiate the financing statement's collateral description. Part IV—the student assignment—applies these lessons as you fill out an actual UCC-1 financing statement.

Part I: Drafting Essentials Explained

An attorney's job here seems ministerial—just filling out the UCC-1 form—but mistakes can be disastrous for clients and attorneys alike. Due diligence on seemingly small matters like getting the names correct and proofreading is as essential as any other aspect of drafting.

A. Attention to Detail[1]

Lawyers are people of the text. Words, numbers, phrases, sentences, paragraphs and sections in contracts, and briefs are their stock in trade. The contracts that you draft must be clear, practical, and precise so that they work. All of that is for your client's sake.

Beyond the client, however, lawyers must pay close attention to detail and take pride in all their work product for their own sake. Each document you create is your calling card. Colleagues, clients, opponents, and courts judge your ability based on your work product. Documents, including correspondence, that contain typos or substantive errors, that are badly formatted, or that do not convey an appearance of well-thought-out precision and accuracy will be held against you in the court of professional reputation. Failure to double-check a filing in secured transactions can cost a client millions of dollars. In the 2015 bankruptcy of General Motors, a careless mistake regarding financing statements led to a $1.5 billion loss to JP Morgan Chase and attendant malpractice exposure for the national firms responsible.[2]

All documents that go out over your name should be proofed, spell-checked, substantively correct, neat, and well-organized. Few people other than lawyers, accountants, editors, and publishers give writing this high level of attention to detail. The effect is cumulative. At some

---

1 George W. Kuney, *Elements of Contract Drafting* 24 (4th ed. 2014) and Haggard & Kuney, *Legal Drafting* 16 (2nd ed. 2007).

2 *In re Motors Liquidation Co.*, 755 F.3d 78 (2d Cir 2015).

point—reached fairly quickly—mistakes add up to the reader, who assumes that the author is (a) not very smart, (b) not very careful, or (c) not paying attention. None of these impressions will advance your legal career. Never rely solely on your word processor's spellchecking software. While spellchecking and grammar checking software can aid drafters, there is no substitute for spending time with your own document, carefully combing through it for spelling, grammatical, and typographical errors. You may even uncover grammatical and word choice errors that have been introduced by your software while in "autocorrect" mode.

B. Clarity and Consistency

Finances often propel clients into a lawyer's office, so keeping track of who gets how much money, when and where and how are central parts of a business transaction. Putting those crucial terms precisely on the page requires clarity and consistency. Drafters generally achieve clarity and consistency by avoiding repetition and making sure that they use the same words the same way throughout the document. For example, once you define First National Bank as "Lender" in the preamble, you should refer to FNB as Lender in the rest of the document. This definition relieves you of reciting the full name of the bank each time you refer to it. This imperative applies in many contexts, and here we focus on the seemingly simple issue of numbers.

1. Numbers

A security agreement should list the principal amount and date of the promissory note it secures only once, when it defines the term "Note." Repeating all of that detail bogs the reader down in needless detail, but more importantly risks ambiguity. Human error increases the chance of a typo every time you list those numbers and dates, and that kind of data is particularly adept at evading even the sharpest proofreader.

Another level of consistency focuses on how you write a number. Amounts can be expressed in either words or numbers, and some drafters use both. For example, a note could provide that "full payment is due ten (10) days after Lender's demand upon Borrower." While that seems protective, it runs another risk. What is the contract term for the date that payment is due if the above provision read, "ten (100) days after...?" As we will see later, principles of contract interpretation make the written-out term prevail when the two differ, so that the term would likely be ten days. But the parties may intend otherwise. Accordingly, many drafting experts recommend that agreements not identify an amount by both letters and numbers.

Another issue in drafting a numerical amount is the different way to state large and small numbers. Drafters tend to follow the rule of using words to state amounts from one to ten, and using numbers to identify amounts from 11 on up. For example:

> *Full payment is due ten days after Lender's demand,*

and

> *Borrower promises to pay $600,000 ("Principal").*

Remember that general rules usually have exceptions. When a numerical amount relates to an essential term of the contract, or reflects a statutory requirement, drafters often use numbers even for small amounts. In the secured transactions context, an endgame provision that gives a debtor a period to cure default may identify the period as "10 days," in part because a reader scanning the page for that information will more quickly find the numbers.

Problem 3: Proofreading

Find and fix the typos and grammatical errors in the following clauses and explain how the error could affect the terms of the contract.

a. The final payment is due five (15) years after the effective date.

b. "Collateral" means all of Borrower's accounts and equipment, not owned or after-acquired.

c. Tenant shall maintain their premises free of dangerous conditions.

C. The Contract Drafting Process[3]

This section provides a description of a typical contracting drafting process, looking first to situations in which your client presents you with a business deal to memorialize and then to situations where you review a contract drafted by the other side.

1. When You Provide the First Draft

For routine commercial transactions, the process often starts with a call or email from a client along the lines of: "We've worked out a deal

---

[3] Excerpted from Sjostrom, *An Introduction to Contract Drafting* 43–52 (2d ed. 2013).

with TCB to supply us with widgets. Draw up the contract, but don't spend a lot of time on it." The client will then give you a rundown of the basic terms of the deal. At this stage, you want to get enough information so that you can prepare a final draft of the contract. The things you will need to know include amount and specification of goods to be provided, price to be paid, transport and delivery details, timing and form of payment, and duration of the deal.

If the client does not provide sufficient detail, ask for it. You should also ask her to forward you any documents relating to the transaction such as a proposal letter or TCB marketing materials. These documents may give you a better sense for what exactly TCB is promising and alert you to aspects of the deal not mentioned by the client that should be reflected in the contract. Additionally, discuss legal fees for the project with the client, ask how quickly the contract needs to be finalized, and when they would like to get the first draft from you. Your goal is to meet or exceed client expectations on cost and timing or explain upfront why those expectations are not reasonable.

Once you have sufficient information to begin drafting, the next step is to locate a form or sample contract (often called a precedent) to use as the starting point for your contract. Rarely, if ever, do lawyers draft contracts from scratch. Instead, they revise and tailor contracts from other deals. Ideally, you have drafted or reviewed a widget contract before that you use as your precedent. If not, ask other attorneys in your firm if they have a sample. If you come up empty, you could check contract form books (available at most law libraries), search contract form databases on Westlaw or Lexis, or do a Google search. The worst case is that you start with a supply contract for some other type of goods, i.e., something other than widgets, and convert it to a widget supply contract. This may involve pulling widget specific language and provisions you located in a form book or a Westlaw/Lexis/Google search. Do not, however, assume that any of the forms or samples you find are well drafted or complete. Once you gain expertise in drafting contracts, you may be surprised by how many poorly drafted contracts are in circulation, including those found in form books and databases. In other words, do not blindly adhere to a precedent or pull language from a form book. To improve your contract's clarity and precision, always scrutinize the language and redraft it as necessary.

For example, a supplier of goods will want to provide minimal express representations and warranties, disclaim implied warranties, cap damages for breach, and limit remedies. Conversely, a buyer will want broad representations and warranties and no warranty disclaimers, no cap on damages, nor limits on remedies. Thus, if you represent the seller, it is best to start with a seller-drafted precedent because it should include warranty disclaimers, a damages cap, etc. Also, it may include seller-favorable provisions that you otherwise would not have thought to include.

Prepare the first draft by revising and tailoring the precedent to reflect your specific deal. Then have your supervising attorney—if any—review the draft and incorporate those changes. Exercise professionalism in responding to these comments by generalizing the corrections. For example, if your supervisor catches a type of error, review the document for similar errors and correct them. So if your reviewer noticed that there were two #6 sections, or a period missing from the end of a heading, double-check the numbering of sections and punctuation of all headings in the agreement. Along the same lines, if your boss or client expresses a preference for listing numbers by both spelling them out and using numerals—contrary to the advice in this chapter—make sure all the numbers are listed the same way. Next, you send your draft to your client for that review and incorporate any comments. Once your client has signed off, send the draft to the other side's attorney.

The other side will get back to you with some comments, which you will then discuss with your client (and perhaps your supervising attorney) and decide how to respond. Revise your draft to reflect the comments

• SKILL: DUE DILIGENCE

from the other side that you have accepted and send the revised draft to the opposing attorney. The standard practice is to send a marked-to-show-changes version (also called a red-line or black-line) and a clean version. You can create a marked-to-show changes version by using the "compare" feature of Microsoft Word.

You and the opposing attorney often negotiate to resolve the comments you rejected. Once you—presumably—resolve all issues, prepare a final version of the contract for the parties to sign.

2. When You Review the Other Party's Draft

Oftentimes, you will not be the one drafting a contract but instead will review one drafted by the other side's attorney. The reviewing process starts similarly to the drafting process with an email or call from the client along the lines of the following: "We've worked out a deal to supply EFG with widgets. Their counsel is drawing up the contract, and she will be forwarding it to you shortly for review. We're anxious to get this finalized, so please turn it around quickly."

The client will then give you a rundown of the business terms of the deal. You need the same type of information you would need if you were drafting the contract so that you know what is supposed to be in the contract. Thus, if the client does not tell you, you should ask the price to be paid, transport and delivery details, etc. Do not assume that the client will review the draft and flag erroneous business terms. For a variety of reasons, clients often do not carefully read draft contracts— if at all—so it is your responsibility to make sure all business terms are correct. Also ask for the name and contact information of the drafting attorney so that you can touch base with her ("Hi, this is _____. I represent TCB on the EFG widget deal. I look forward to working with you . . ."), to comply with your client's desire "to get this finalized." Further, as you would do when drafting, ask the client to forward you any documents relating to the transaction (e.g., proposal letters, marketing materials) to give you a better understanding of the deal and documents that opposing counsel has.

While waiting for the first draft to hit your inbox, secure one or more sample contracts of similar deals, preferably early drafts prepared by seller's counsel since you represent the seller in this deal. Reading through them will give you a sense of standard provisions for these types of deals. More importantly, reading through samples will help you spot seller-favorable provisions that the drafter of the contract has left out. Recall that parties are often diametrically opposed on various issues. For example, EFG's attorney is unlikely to include in the draft a disclaimer of the implied warranty of merchantability because it is to her client's advantage for it not to be disclaimed. You may have forgotten about UCC § 2–314,[4] but your memory will be jogged when reading a sample contract that includes a warranty disclaimer, and you will then have sample language to suggest so that a revision disclaims the warranty.

There is no standard way to review a draft. Most people develop their own styles. Here is one style, which may work for you and will at least give you a sense of the review process.

1. Give the draft a quick read upon receipt to get a sense for how well it is drafted and how it is organized. The main objective here is to assess how much time you will need to work through it.

2. Scrutinize the draft line by line, noting drafting errors, ambiguities, inconsistencies, typos, etc. A good way to do this is to print the draft and handwrite changes on it much as a proofreader does. Attorneys call this "marking up" a draft.

---

4   UCC § 2–314 provides, in relevant part: "Unless excluded or modified (Section 2–316), a warranty that the goods shall be merchantable is implied in a contract for their sale if the seller is a merchant with respect to goods of that kind."

In fact, some attorneys use the standard proofreader's marks for this step, which are set out in exercise #2 on security agreement front matter and also should pop up in a web search for "proofreader marks."

3. Give the draft another close read, but this time focus on what is missing. Draft language for provisions you want added. Some attorneys will simply write "add implied warranty disclaimer" on a draft. The problem with this approach is that it might not be clear to the drafter what exactly you want, or she may use language that does not go as far as you want. It is best to type up language that you want added in a separate Word document as opposed to handwriting it on the draft. Label each provision sequentially as "Rider 1," "Rider 2," etc. and indicate on the draft where you want each rider inserted.[5]

4. If the draft contains complicated, specialized provisions—i.e., those addressing intellectual property, tax, or employee benefits—consider having someone with expertise in the relevant area review them.

5. Set the draft aside for a day and then give it another close read to make sure that you caught everything. Fresh eyes can catch typos and other defects that your eyes skim over when you have been reviewing the document for a long time.

The next step is to share your mark-up with the client and your supervising attorney (if applicable) to see if they have any questions or thoughts regarding your comments or comments of their own to add. You may want to include a cover memo for the client to draw attention to particular sections or ask specific questions.

---

5   A rider is an additional writing that is attached to a document to modify it.

Once the client and supervising attorney sign off, transmit your comments to the other side. If you email a PDF of your mark-up along with a Word file of your riders, the drafter may just copy and paste the riders into the contract. Depending on the extent and complexity of the comments, you may then do a conference call with the drafter to walk through them. Some reviewing attorneys do formal comment memos specifying and explaining each comment, but this method can be inefficient because the memo takes a long time to draft and usually comments on the mark-up are self-explanatory, especially to an experienced drafter. Thus check with your client or supervising attorney to see if you should write the memo. As an alternative to a formal memo, you can include an explanation of comments that you think may be controversial or confusing in the body of the email that transmits the mark-up.

As mentioned above, the drafter will make changes to the contract in response to your comments and undoubtedly will reject some of them. You will then get feedback from your client as to whether to push for one or more of the rejected changes and proceed accordingly. A client will normally ask what you think on pushing for a particular comment, so think through your answer and reasoning in advance.

While this brief explanation should help get you started, you learn by reading, drafting and editing contracts, not by reading articles or books about contract drafting. Because you do not do much of that in law school, no one expects you to be great at drafting right out of school. What you learn here and in the other exercises will help you draft respectable contracts from day one and accelerate your learning curve towards becoming a contract drafting expert.

Part II: Legal Rules and Search Exercise

UCC § 9–502 requires that a financing statement have three minimum elements to be enforceable and § 9–516 adds several that are necessary for the filing office to accept the financing statement.

A. Explanation: Financing Statement Sufficiency and Filing Requirements

Bare sufficiency under § 9–502 requires only that the financing statement include (1) the debtor's name; (2) the secured party's name; and (3) a collateral description. UCC § 9–503 tells filers how to properly identify a debtor based on whether that debtor is a registered organization (i.e., a corporation or LLC), a non-registered organization such as a partnership, or an individual. UCC § 9–504 provides a standard for identifying the collateral that is more lenient than the UCC § 9–108 test for describing collateral in a security agreement, in large part because § 9–502(d) allows secured parties to file a financing statement at the very outset of negotiations with a debtor, when the parties have not yet precisely identified the collateral that will secure debtor's obligation to the creditor.

UCC § 9–516 provides additional requirements that a financing statement must satisfy to be accepted by the filing office , such as providing addresses for the parties and indicating whether the debtor is an organization or an individual.

UCC §§ 9–301 and 9–307 dictate the state in which a creditor should file a financing statement, which is also where searchers should to look for other financing statements encumbering a potential debtor's personal property. The general rule is to file where the debtor is located. Here, the debtor is in New York.

B. Application: Search UCC Files

In many states, financing statements are filed in the Secretary of State's office, but in New York, that office is called the Department of State, Division of Corporations. Its web address is http://www.dos.ny.gov/corps/uccforms.html.

Before FNB lends money to Bolt's Urban Hardware, the bank wants to know whether the store's property is already encumbered. Thus, your assignment is to search the New York UCC files for other financing statements that reveal lenders that FNB would have to buy out to enjoy top priority to the collateral.

Assume for purposes of this exercise and the remaining security agreement exercises that Bianca Bolt has two brothers. David Bolt lives on Pinner Road in Cherry Creek, NY, and Gregory Bolt lives on County Line Road in Watkins Glen, NY. Until last year, Bianca, David and Gregory together collected and sold vintage and antique ironwork. They kept it their homes and also in a warehouse under an account in Bianca Bolt's name. FNB may take a security interest in the part of the ironwork collection that the hardware store has an interest in.

Search the UCC files in New York to see if any financing statements trigger further inquiries by FNB or suggest the advisability of particular representations and warranties in exercise #4. Be sure to note the date that any relevant financing statement was filed, which is indicated by a stamp in the upper right hand corner. Also note whether the financing statement has lapsed or been continued, and what collateral it covers. Article 9 generally gives priority to the creditor who is the first to file or otherwise perfect its security interest in the collateral.

Part III: Negotiate Collateral Description

The next step is to determine the central financing statement term: the collateral.

A. Negotiation Essentials Explained

An "anchor" in a negotiation is the first number or other item that one of the negotiators proposes. Here, if FNB proposes that the financing statement describe the collateral as "all of debtor's personal property," that anchor greases the tracks for most or all of debtor's property to serve as collateral. Likewise, if debtor's counsel proposes language such as "all of debtor's inventory and equipment," that narrow description would increase the chance that much less of debtor's property will secure the loan. The following excerpt from Harvard Law School's Program on Negotiation explains the benefits and dangers of intentional anchoring.

> **PON Staff, Integrative Negotiation Examples:**
> **Effective Anchors as First Offers, Sept. 5, 2016**[6]
>
> People tend to irrationally fixate on the first number put forth in a negotiation—the anchor—no matter how arbitrary it may be. Even when we know the anchor has limited relevance, we fail to sufficiently adjust our judgments away from it. Here are some integrative negotiation examples providing negotiation techniques for effective anchoring at the bargaining table.
>
> It is desirable to anchor first in many negotiations, for several reasons. In many negotiation scenarios, you are trying to both learn about the "zone of possible agreement" (ZOPA) and influence the other side's

---

6   Available at http://www.pon.harvard.edu/daily/negotiation-skills-daily/effective-anchors-as-first-offers/

perception of the ZOPA. While advance research can help you reduce your uncertainty about the ZOPA, you typically will have more to learn about the ZOPA once talks begin. As such, you will be vulnerable to being anchored. Therefore, anchoring first in price-oriented negotiations can be both good offense and good defense.

An overly aggressive offer, however, risks derailing negotiations if it causes the other side to question your credibility or to wonder whether negotiated agreement is even possible. Because it is hard to know what your counterpart will view as absurd, anchoring with a relatively inflexible, extreme offer increases the probability of reaching a stalemate. Anchoring instead with a flexible but extreme offer gives you a lower-risk opportunity to favorably shape your counterpart's perceptions of the ZOPA.

The most effective anchors further reduce risk because, rather than placing firm offers on the table, they merely introduce relevant numbers. A job applicant may state his belief that people with his qualifications tend to be paid between $85,000 and $95,000 annually, or he might mention that a former colleague just received an offer of $92,000. This assertion is not an offer; it's an anchor that affects the other side's perceptions of the ZOPA.

Finally, you can also anchor by citing apparently comparable negotiated agreements as precedent. Consider the case of a money manager preparing to negotiate her annual bonus. "While bonuses last year were 50% of salary," she might tell her boss, "I recognize that this year will not be as good as last year." Another approach is to mention proposals made by more extreme elements of one's constituency. A prospective customer might tell a salesperson that, while he loves the product, his purchasing department is undoubtedly going to demand price cuts of 15% or more. Such statements can have an anchoring effect without requiring you to make an extreme offer that could jeopardize talks. As these integrative negotiation examples have shown, sometimes revealing one's hand is the quickest route to value creation at the bargaining table.

Consider how the debtor and FNB will use this information as you plan how to negotiate what collateral is listed on the financing statement.

B. Negotiation Applied to the Collateral Description

Now you are ready to negotiate the collateral description in the financing statement. Before you start to negotiate consider what the debtor and FNB would each like as a starting proposal and ideal collateral description, and why. Be prepared to counter the other side's argument for a broader or more narrow description.

Part IV: Student Assignment: Draft Financing Statement

Now it is time to fill in the blanks on a UCC-1 financing statement. Usually the secured party does this task since it protects the creditor's interests, but you should fill it out as a team. Download the UCC-1 form from the book website.

A: Template: UCC-1 Financing Statement

UCC FINANCING STATEMENT
FOLLOW INSTRUCTIONS

A. NAME & PHONE OF CONTACT AT FILER (optional)

B. E-MAIL CONTACT AT FILER (optional)

C. SEND ACKNOWLEDGMENT TO: (Name and Address)

THE ABOVE SPACE IS FOR FILING OFFICE USE ONLY

1. DEBTOR'S NAME: Provide only <u>one</u> Debtor name (1a or 1b) (use exact, full name; do not omit, modify, or abbreviate any part of the Debtor's name); if any part of the Individual Debtor's name will not fit in line 1b, leave all of item 1 blank, check here ☐ and provide the Individual Debtor information in item 10 of the Financing Statement Addendum (Form UCC1Ad)

1a. ORGANIZATION'S NAME			
1b. INDIVIDUAL'S SURNAME	FIRST PERSONAL NAME	ADDITIONAL NAME(S)/INITIAL(S)	SUFFIX
1c. MAILING ADDRESS	CITY	STATE POSTAL CODE	COUNTRY

OR

2. DEBTOR'S NAME: Provide only <u>one</u> Debtor name (2a or 2b) (use exact, full name; do not omit, modify, or abbreviate any part of the Debtor's name); if any part of the Individual Debtor's name will not fit in line 2b, leave all of item 2 blank, check here ☐ and provide the Individual Debtor information in item 10 of the Financing Statement Addendum (Form UCC1Ad)

2a. ORGANIZATION'S NAME			
2b. INDIVIDUAL'S SURNAME	FIRST PERSONAL NAME	ADDITIONAL NAME(S)/INITIAL(S)	SUFFIX
2c. MAILING ADDRESS	CITY	STATE POSTAL CODE	COUNTRY

OR

3. SECURED PARTY'S NAME (or NAME of ASSIGNEE of ASSIGNOR SECURED PARTY): Provide only <u>one</u> Secured Party name (3a or 3b)

3a. ORGANIZATION'S NAME			
3b. INDIVIDUAL'S SURNAME	FIRST PERSONAL NAME	ADDITIONAL NAME(S)/INITIAL(S)	SUFFIX
3c. MAILING ADDRESS	CITY	STATE POSTAL CODE	COUNTRY

OR

4. COLLATERAL: This financing statement covers the following collateral:

5. Check <u>only</u> if applicable and check <u>only</u> one box: Collateral is ☐ held in a Trust (see UCC1Ad, item 17 and Instructions)   ☐ being administered by a Decedent's Personal Representative

6a. Check <u>only</u> if applicable and check <u>only</u> one box:
☐ Public-Finance Transaction   ☐ Manufactured-Home Transaction   ☐ A Debtor is a Transmitting Utility

6b. Check <u>only</u> if applicable and check <u>only</u> one box:
☐ Agricultural Lien   ☐ Non-UCC Filing

7. ALTERNATIVE DESIGNATION (if applicable): ☐ Lessee/Lessor   ☐ Consignee/Consignor   ☐ Seller/Buyer   ☐ Bailee/Bailor   ☐ Licensee/Licensor

8. OPTIONAL FILER REFERENCE DATA:

FILING OFFICE COPY — UCC FINANCING STATEMENT (Form UCC1) (Rev. 04/20/11)

International Association of Commercial Administrators (IACA)

B. Tips for Saving the UCC-1 Form with Data Included

Your computer's operating system can make it easier or more difficult to save a copy of your financing statement. These tips apply if your copy of the UCC-1 form is a fillable PDF. Follow these instructions if you have problems with the text disappearing from the fields after you save, or the recipient gets a blank form.

If you retrieve the form from a website, first download the form from the website. Do not complete the fillable PDF within your internet browser.

1. For Mac users:

If you use Preview, once you complete the form, click on File → "Export as PDF" from the dropdown menu, then save the file under a new name. You will not be able to make changes after exporting, but you can go back to the original PDF to make changes and export again.

If you still have difficulties, download the latest version of Adobe Acrobat Reader DC for free from the Adobe website. Open the form in Reader, fill out the form and save.

2. For PC users:

You will need the latest version of either Adobe Acrobat Pro, Adobe Acrobat Reader DC (for Windows 7 and higher) or Adobe Reader XI or higher. Open your Adobe program and go to File → "Open" to open the file from where you saved it. After filling out the form, go to File → "Print." Change the printer to Adobe PDF, Save as PDF, or a similar PDF printer. Save the file under a new name. You will not be able to make changes after "printing," but you can go back to the original PDF to make changes and "print" again.

Security Agreement Essentials
Skill: Identify and Draft a Contract's Most Important Terms

Overview

THE PROMISSORY NOTE and financing statement assignments in exercises #1 and #3 covered the drafting skills of filling in two types of forms, and exercise #2 required you to create a framework for the security agreement's substantive provisions. As a doctrinal matter, exercise #1 memorialized the debt that is secured through the security agreement, exercise #2 constructed the skeleton for a legally binding security agreement, and exercise #3 established FNB's place in line for a priority contest.

Having laid that foundation, you are ready to dive into the heart of this transaction.

This exercise may be the most important in this book. Doctrinally, it covers the crucial task of making sure that a security interest attaches. In terms of drafting, it is the first exercise that closely pairs the lessons of contract drafting with substantive provisions of Article 9. You will negotiate the key terms of the security agreement—collateral and obligation clauses—then edit the template to ensure that the writing conforms with the three attachment requirements of UCC § 9-203. If a transaction fails because you forget to have the debtor sign, or because you describe the collateral as "all of Debtor's personal property" in violation of UCC § 9-108, FNB has no security interest and is left with the very modest rights of an unsecured creditor. Should you represent the lender, you may have lost your client and even your job if the amount at stake is sufficiently large.

The skill developed here involves identifying and drafting a contract's most important terms. In a security agreement, that means understanding how doctrinal rules like the definitions in UCC § 9–102 provide an efficient way to precisely and clearly describe collateral, and how to draft after-acquired property and future advance clauses. Precision in after-acquired property clauses requires facility with grammatical norms such as comma placement and drafting norms of tabulation. Negotiating and drafting what obligation is secured hammers home the different functions of after-acquired property and future advance clauses as well as the basic fact that a security interest creates a link between a debtor's property and an obligation.

Part I covers drafting essentials on formatting and canons of construction. Part II applies those lessons as you negotiate what collateral secures what obligation(s). Part III recaps Article 9 rules that dictate how to reduce the agreement you have reached to words on the page, and Part IV pulls it all together with the assignment of editing the security agreement template to reflect the terms of your negotiated agreement.

Part I: Contract Drafting Essentials Explained

This section covers two drafting topics: formatting details like tabulation and section numbering and substantive material on how to draft a list that avoids problems of contract interpretation under canons of construction such as *expressio univs* and *ejusdem generis*.[1]

---

[1] *Expressio univs est exclusio alterius* translates to "to express one thing is to exclude another," and can create problems for a creditor that enumerates items of collateral but leaves out an item that it intended to cover. *Ejusdem generis* means "of the same kind or nature," and can limit a list of collateral to others in the same category.

A. Formatting[2]

Appearances matter. Lawyers, business people and courts expect lawyer-drafted agreements to adhere to formatting and stylistic conventions. Moreover, these conventions often serve to make a contract easier to read and understood by readers like your clients who may not be lawyers themselves.

The readability of the document is enhanced by lots of white space, referring to the spaces on the page where nothing is printed. The drafter should make a conscious effort to avoid producing a document in which every square centimeter is filled with text. For example, look at this page. Each section is single spaced, with blank lines and bolded headings between the provisions. Tabulation, covered below, also prevents solid blocks of text from getting in the way of readability.

1. Type Size and Font

Text should be no smaller than 12 points. Indeed, some appellate court rules require that briefs be in 14-point type, and contract drafters would be wise to emulate that rule, in at least two situations. First, if the document will be frequently referred to during the term of the agreement—particularly if it will be used on a construction site or the shop floor—it should not require a magnifying glass to read it. Conversely, type size is not that important if the document will simply establish a legal relationship and then be filed away, resurrected only if the transaction fails and litigation ensues. Second, an adequate type size is especially important in consumer-oriented documents, where state and federal statutes make easy readability a condition of enforceability. For example, one court held that a portion of an installment

---

2   Based on from Haggard and Kuney, *Legal Drafting* 335–336; 337–338; 339–341; 344 (2d ed. 2007).

sales contract that was printed in 8-point type rather than the required 10-point type violated the Truth in Lending Act.[3] Standard real estate contracts, which in many respects represent drafting at its worst, are often crammed into the seemingly mandatory two-page (front and back of a standard piece of paper), densely packed, tiny print format that defies reading or comprehension.[4]

Choose a typeface that is easy to read, usually a member of the Times family. This sentence is printed in Times New Roman. `Avoid type-faces such as Courier, which is a holdover from the days of type written legal documents,` and sans serif typefaces like Arial which are modern but tiresome in lengthy documents. *Do not even consider any kind of script or cursive font, even for the heading of the document, because it is difficult to read.*

2. All Capitals and Underlining

Type that is set in upper and lower case is easier to read than to type in all capitals, and underlined text is a strain to the eyes. Back when most contracts were typewritten, all caps and underlining were the only way to set off the headings and provide emphasis to select portions of the text. Hence, you might have seen something like this.

---

3   *Leon v. Family Fitness Center*, 71 Cal.Rptr 2d 923 (Cal. App. 4th 1998). More recent regulations promulgated by the Consumer Financial Protection Bureau make font and type size relevant re: conspicuousness requirements. *See also* Truth in Lending Act-RESPA, explained at https://www.consumerfinance.gov/eregulations/1026-Subpart-B-Interp/2015-18239#1026-5-a-1-Interp-1.

4   *See, e.g.,* http://www.amortgage.com/xSites/Mortgage/AlexanderMortgageCorp/Content/Uploaded-Files/P%20and%20S%20Residential.pdf.

> *T. DISCLAIMER OF WARRANTIES. Except as provided in paragraphs c, q, and r above, THIS PECAN SHELLER IS SOLD WITHOUT ANY WARRANTIES, EXPRESS OR IMPLIED, INCLUDING THE WARRANTY OF MERCHANTABILITY AND OF FITNESS FOR ANY PARTICULAR USE AND ANY PRIOR REPRESENTATIONS BY SELLER, ORAL OR IN WRITING, TO THE CONTRARY ARE VOID.*

Today—absent statutory requirements to the contrary—the better practice to satisfy conspicuousness requirements is to use bolded headings with a font-size two points larger than the rest of the text and bolded phrases for the critical words.

> *Another way to satisfy conspicuousness requirements is to put the required language in a text box like this one.*

3. Justification

Some believe that full left and right justification not only makes for a neater looking text, it also makes paragraph breaks more distinct, thus contributing to the comprehensibility of the document.

But not everyone agrees. One source of the disagreement is the Securities and Exchange Commission (SEC), so drafters of documents with that agency as an audience should take note. Although it is only a recommendation, the SEC and many practicing attorneys believe left-only justified text is easier to read, because fully justified text has uneven spacing between the words. Those gaps can be minimized by the use of short words (a desirable trait in drafting), the automatic hyphenation feature of the word processor, and standard rather than column-length lines. The jury is still out on this issue and templates from which you borrow provisions may have justified margins. Make justification a conscious choice and proofread carefully to make sure that justification is consistent throughout the document.

4. Numbered Pages

Even a short document should be page numbered. Usually, a simple "5" or "-5-" at the bottom of the page is sufficient. But some drafters, exercising caution in important documents and to ensure that no page is later removed, use the "Page 5 of 100 pages" convention. Often these documents also provide a space for the initials of the parties on each page. It would be pretentious, however, to use these conventions on an ordinary house painting contract.

5. Numbered or Lettered Paragraph Headings

Numbered or lettered paragraph headings provide visual signposts in a document. They make it easy for the reader to find a particular provision and they give the top-to-bottom reader an indication of what the next provision is about. A document without them burdens the reader with a vexatious and tedious reading experience.

The headings and subheadings reflect the organization that the drafter has decided upon. Indeed, an inability to produce the necessary heading and subheadings and an improper outlining structure are sure signs of faulty organization.

Some drafters prefer this type of numbering format:

> I. *Seller's Obligations*
>> A. *Delivery*
>>> 1. *Method*
>>> 2. *Time*
>>> 3. *Place*
>> B. *Installation*

Others prefer to do it this way:

> *§1 Seller's Obligations*
>   *§1.1 Delivery*
>   *§ 1.1.1 Mode*
>   *§1.1.2 Time*
>   *§1.1.3 Place*
>   *§1.2 Installation*

The numbers or letters make it easy for the parties to refer to specific sections and allow for clear cross-reference within the document itself. However, after the document is complete, the drafter should double check all cross-references. In an early version of the document, the referenced material may have been in paragraph I(B)(3)(a). In the final version of the document the material may appear in 1(B)(4)(a). Unless the cross-reference is changed, the document will be confusing, at best. Indeed, an erroneous cross-reference could make the document ambiguous or produce unintended results. You can minimize the danger of an erroneous numerical cross reference by also including the paragraph heading in the cross-reference, in the hope that the referenced subject matter will prevail over the referenced number. While word processing programs automatically link cross-references across a document, that tactic is no substitute for careful proofreading.

The headings must accurately reflect the content of the paragraph. A drafter should not, for example, bury a warranty disclaimer in a paragraph marked "Warranties." Such a disclaimer may not even be legally effective due to lack of conspicuousness.

Some drafters are inclined to include a provision stating that headings are not part of the contract and should not be used to limit, expand, or interpret the substantive text. That provision essentially admits to sloppy drafting. The better approach is to word the heading so that it is consistent with the substantive text that follows. The drafter's inability to do this easily may indicate a fundamental flaw in the document's conceptualization or organization.

6. Tabbing

Drafters often use a device called tabbing to avoid ambiguities of modification. Consider the following provision written in conventional paragraph form:

> *A person who drives an automobile on a public road recklessly, negligently, or at a speed or in a manner posing a danger to others* **considering the condition of the highway and the weather** *is guilty of a misdemeanor.*

Does the bolded language only modify the dangerous manner of the driving? Or does it also modify "recklessly," "negligently," and "at a speed"? Grammarians generally hold that a clause modifies the material that immediately precedes it.

To see how this works, consider which items must be organic in the following covenant: "Seller shall deliver coffee, tea and milk sourced by an organic farmer." Because the clause "sourced by an organic farmer" comes at the end of the provision, grammatical rules dictate that the clause modifies only the noun immediately before it. In other words, the covenant would require Seller to deliver organic milk, but would allow for the delivery of conventional or non-organic coffee and tea. To require that coffee, tea, and milk all be organic, a drafter could edit the clause to insert a comma and "all" after milk. The clarified clause would read, "Seller shall deliver coffee, tea, and milk, all sourced from organic farmers."

Tabulation provides another way to write precisely. The organic coffee, tea, and milk provision could read as follows:

> *Seller shall deliver*
>> *coffee,*
>> *tea, and*
>> *milk*
> *sourced by organic farmers*

By bringing the "sourced" phrase back over to the left margin of the section, the drafter indicates that it modifies all three of the tabbed items. As you draft the collateral description of your security agreement, make sure that the phrase "now-owned or whenever acquired" is placed to unambiguously indicate that it modifies the collateral that the parties intend to be covered. Tabulation provides one method of achieving this clarity, and another is to place the phrase at the beginning of the list. Here, that method would rewrite the clause to read, "Seller shall deliver the following goods sourced by organic farmers: coffee, tea, and milk." Placing the clause before the colon and at the beginning of the list makes clear that the organic requirement applies to all the items on the list.

B. Drafting a List

A list of items that the parties intend to be collateral is the backbone of many security agreements. Drafters of all kinds of documents catalog items, generally using two formats: a list and an enumeration. Either one is acceptable for your security agreement.

1. Two Ways to Format a List

A list consists of an introductory sentence that expresses the nature of the relationship between the items in the list by indicating whether the items are cumulative or alternative. For example, if the sentence is imposing a duty, the sentence should indicate whether the holder of the duty is required to satisfy all of the items on the list or only one. The introductory sentence may end with a colon or a period. Each item in the list begins with a capital letter and ends with a period. The items should be numbered, lettered, or introduced with a bullet or other visual representation.

Here is an example of a cumulative list:

> **B. Appliances.** *Landlord shall furnish the following appliances and maintain them in good working order:*
>
> 1. *Refrigerator.*
> 2. *Stove.*
> 3. *Disposal.*
> 4. *Washer.*
> 5. *Dryer.*

Here is a list of alternatives:

> **IV. Verification.** *An applicant must verify citizenship status by supplying one or more of the following documents:*
>
> A. *Birth certificate.*
> B. *Driver's license.*
> C. *Social Security card.*
> D. *Department of State certificate.*

Another way to list items in a series is in the form of enumeration. Unlike a list, an enumeration retains its single-sentence structure. The introductory clause may have no terminal punctuation at all, although some drafters use dashes and colons. Each item in the enumeration is terminated with a comma or a semi-colon, except the last one, which takes a period. The nature of the relationship between the items in the series is indicated by an "and" or an "or" following the next to last item. A single "and" or "or" following the penultimate item in the series is sufficient; it is not necessary to put the connective after each item in the series. The enumeration can be accomplished with parenthesized numbers or letters (for ease of reference) or simple bullets. For example:

> *Agent's territory consists of*
>
> - *All of South Carolina, except the counties of Greenville, Richland, Horrey, and Charleston;*
>
> - *All of Georgia, except the City of Atlanta; and*
>
> - *North Carolina.*

It gets more complicated when you consider the substantive content of the list. Two canons of contract interpretation address the danger that a court or other reader of your agreement will read the list to exclude items that you meant to include: *expressio unius* and *ejusdem generis*. Two additional interpretive rules about the relation of letters and numbers, and general and specific provisions, will also help you achieve the drafting goal of precision.

Problem 4: Formatting for Clarity and Readability

Reformat and edit the following collateral description to make it more clear and readable. **Hint:** legalese contributes to the clutter.

"Collateral" shall mean all of the personal property of the Borrower, all whether now owned or existing or hereafter acquired or created and wherever situated, and shall include, without limitation, the following: (a) All inventory, and all warranties, licenses, franchises, and general intangibles related thereto (including, without limitation, software) and all returned, rejected or repossessed goods . . .

2. Canons of Construction

Students are often surprised to learn that a creditor can be better off with a simple list of collateral than a long detailed one. UCC § 9–102 provides detailed definitions that describe any kind of personal property, so "all accounts, now-owned and whenever acquired" is unambiguous, while "accounts receivable from sales made subsequent to the closing date" can and did lead to litigation.[5]

---

5 *Stoumbos v. Kilimnik*, 988 F.2d 949 (9th Cir. 1993).

a. *Expressio Unius*[6]

Expressio unius is shorthand for a Latin phrase that means "the expression of one thing is the exclusion of another." This rule creates an inference that when a document lists certain things, it excludes others. In *Citizen's Bank and Trust v. Gibson Lumber*,[7] a secured party had to litigate whether its collateral description of "all sawmill equipment" followed by a list of twenty-one items also covered three pieces of equipment that were not on the list. These items, central to the mill's operation, were large enough to require their own building.

Lenders pay drafters to avoid that ambiguity. The lawyers may have believed they were protecting their client by detailed descriptions of some items (i.e., "Lumber grading shed, rips, gangs, saws, decks and miscellaneous equipment") but "all sawmill equipment, now-owned and whenever acquired" would have worked better.

If you intend a list to be exclusive, state that expressly. If you intend the list to be non-exclusive, then say that. One way to signal that the list includes additional items is catch-all language such as "and all others." This fix, however, can also be dangerous, as the next rule demonstrates.

b. *Ejusdem Generis*

When a sentence lists several specific items and concludes with a catch-all phrase like "all other," the rule of *ejusdem generis*—meaning "of the same kind"—provides that the general phrase is limited by the specific words that precede it. Courts apply the rule by identifying the common denominator of the specified items and then limiting "others" to entities that possess that characteristic. The Federal Arbitration Act, for example, provides as follows:

---

6   Sections on canons of construction based on Haggard & Kuney, *Legal Drafting* 74–79 & 242."

7   96 B.R. 751 (Bankr. W.D. Ky. 1989).

> *Nothing herein contained shall apply to contracts of seamen, railroad employees, or any other class of workers engaged in foreign or interstate commerce.*

As a matter of constitutional law, foreign or interstate commerce is an extremely broad concept, covering even the farmer who grows grain for consumption by his own cattle. But for the purposes of this act, the courts have construed the phrase as excluding from coverage only workers who share a salient characteristic of those listed—namely, being literally engaged in the interstate transportation industry, like seamen and railway employees. A farmer's contract with a laborer to harvest wheat for local consumption would thus not be governed by the Arbitration Act.

The problem with the technique of finding the common denominator is that a collection of items may have several common denominators. For example, "automobiles, trucks and buses" have all the following common characteristics: (1) they are generally driven by an internal combustion engine; (2) they operate primarily on public streets and highways; (3) they operate on land; and (4) they have rubber wheels. So what would the phrase "and similar vehicles" cover? It depends on what the operative common denominator is. If it is (1), then a horse drawn carriage is excluded, although it would not be excluded under the other categories. If the common denominator is (2), then a golf cart or dune buggy is excluded, but again not under the others. If it is (3), then boats and airplanes are excluded. If it is (4), then a vintage World War II tank is excluded, although it would not be excluded under (1) or (3).

To determine what is included or excluded by the phrase "and similar vehicles," a court would be required to determine the intended common denominator. But the drafter should not casually surrender this power to a court. It is the drafter's function, not the court's, to identify express terms. When a court applies the rule of *ejusdem generis* it evidences bad drafting.

Some drafters, moreover, make the situation even worse by adding a phrase like: "or other vehicles [or whatever], without limitation or restriction to the generality of the foregoing." All this edit does is give the courts a complete wild card in determining what is or is not included in the provision.

3. Tips for Skirting Problems with *Expressio Unius* and *Ejusdem Generis*

Ask: do I really need each of these terms? Will fewer do? If *expressio unis* may be a problem, consider using a more general term that contains within its meaning all desired alternatives. "Transfer," for example, may cover "sell, transfer, alienate and dispose of."

Do not tuck in a general reference such as "etc." or "and the like" at the end of a list to cure the problem.

4. Written Amounts Prevail Over Arabic Number Amounts

Under the rule, if a contract provides that the price is "two thousand, five hundred and fifty-six dollars and eighty-nine cents ($42,557.89)," the lower spelled-out price generally prevails. Yet modern courts would probably ignore the rule to avoid an outcome that is grossly unfair or clearly inconsistent with the intent of the parties. But if the difference was limited to the "… fifty-six" versus "57" portion of the price, a court would probably follow the rule and treat the "fifty-six" as legally binding.

The idea is that a bad actor can more easily change a number (for example, making a 1 into a 4, or moving a decimal point) than change letters that spell out a dollar amount in promissory note or check. But the rule also seems to run counter to studies showing that most people confronted with both the spelled-out and the numerical version of an amount read only the numerical version. Whether or not the numerals reflect the mutual understanding of the parties, courts are likely to apply the rule that amounts written in letters prevail over number amounts.

The drafter can avoid the implication of this rule by simply presenting all dollar numbers in the numerical form, and making sure that all the zeros and commas are correct. Numbers that do not reflect dollar amounts should be in either the spelled-out or numerical form—but not both. Some lawyers have moved to using just numbers to avoid potential confusion. For young lawyers, probably the most important thing is to understand the need to be consistent and the preference of your supervising lawyers.

5. Specific Language Prevails Over General Language or Provisions

This rule means that the more specific provisions control when a statute or private law document or a provision within those documents deals with a subject in general terms and another document or provision deals with the subject in a specific and detailed way. Thus, the drafter should be aware of any statute or agreement between the same parties that deals with the same subject matter and should make the relationship between the statutes or documents express, rather than relying on the court's invocation of this rule.

Part II: Negotiation

Negotiate the collateral and obligations with the lawyer representing the other side. Consider whether to cover after-acquired collateral, and whether the obligation is just the promissory note or other obligations as well.

If your professor provides handouts that convey instructions from your client, remember your professional obligations to keep communications with your client confidential. Do not tell your bargaining partner representing the other party what your client told you except as necessary to follow your client's instructions.

Part III: Legal Rules

A key part of this assignment is complying with UCC § 9–203's requirement that the security agreement "describe" the collateral. The description must identify the property associated with the store (i.e., equipment or accounts) but not Bianca Bolt's own property because Bianca is not signing the security agreement in her individual capacity. Each team must puzzle out what UCC § 9–102 terms describe the items of property that could be collateral, and also whether any special rules apply to that description under UCC §§ 9–108 or 9–204. Remember that the debtor is an LLC and cannot, by definition, own or control consumer goods.

Part IV: Student Assignment: Negotiate and Draft Collateral and Obligation Provisions

You are now ready to draft and properly format the core business provisions of the security agreement. These provisions are like the engine in a car—without them, the contract cannot get the parties where they want to go.

Edit the template below, which is also available in downloadable form on the book website. Provisions that we will address in future exercises, such as events of default, are deleted and indicated only with brackets and brief headings. It is the same template used in exercise #2 except that clearer language has replaced much of the legalese.

• SKILL: IDENTIFY AND DRAFT A CONTRACT'S MOST IMPORTANT TERMS

The action clauses at issue cover five business issues:

- FNB's agreement to lend money to the debtor;

- The debtor's promise to execute a promissory note to memorialize the debt;

- A definition of the collateral secures that debt;

- A definition of the obligation(s) that the collateral secures; and

- Facts that are necessary to create a security interest in the described collateral.

Applicable contract concepts are declarations (i.e., definitions and the creation of the security interest), representations and warranties (i.e., a statements that the debtor owns the collateral), and covenants (i.e., the debtor's promise to execute the promissory note).

A. Tips for the Exercise

- Comply with all doctrinal requirements for enforceability. Though § 9–203 only requires Bianca Bolt's signature as Managing Member of the LLC, you should include both parties' signatures.

- Consider creating a definitions article that defines collateral and obligations.

- Consider whether and how to include property that the debtor will acquire after the parties sign this security agreement.

- Consider whether you can simplify the obligations definition. Have you included attorney's fees as a secured obligation?

- Consider the document's organization. Do you want to place the debtor's representation and warranty about owning the collateral in the creation of the security interest section or in a separate section with the debtor's other representations and warranties?

B. Checklist for Format

❑ Font is Tahoma, Times New Roman or comparable

❑ Font size is 12 point

❑ Article headings use Roman numerals, centered, boldface

❑ Section headings have either numbers or a mix of numbers and letters. Key decimal point numbers to Article numbers (e.g., § 3.01 is the first section in Article III); boldface

❑ Heading of section is indented after section number; boldface

❑ Headings—initial caps of key words

❑ Pages are numbered

❑ Signature lines appear on a page with some substantive text

C. Template: Security Agreement

Here is the template. Either cut and paste from the front matter and end matter that you passed in for exercise #2 or refer back to the term sheet in the Introduction or documents produced in earlier exercises to be sure you properly identify the debtor and creditor and properly format the signature blocks to reflect that agents (Bianca Bolt and Lamar Lee) sign on behalf of the debtor and the bank.

LOAN AND SECURITY AGREEMENT

THIS LOAN AND SECURITY AGREEMENT (the "**Agreement**") is made June 12, 2017, between SECOND BANK OF SPRINGFIELD (the "**Lender**"), a corporation located at 123 Fake St., Springfield, NY 13333, and GLOBAL PAINT & HARDWARE, Inc. (d/b/a Global Club Hardware), a New York corporation (the "**Borrower**"), located at 747 Hammer Dr., Shelbyville, NY 13332.

RECITALS

A. Borrower operates a Club Hardware store (the "Business") at the same location as the Borrower's address above (the "**Business Premises**").

B. Borrower has applied to the Lender for a Loan in the original principal amount of $350,000 (the "**Loan**").

C. Lender is willing to provide the Loan if Borrower enters this Agreement to secure the Loan.

THEREFORE, in consideration of their mutual promises, the parties agree as follows:

   1.   [Interpretation.]

   2.   The Loan.

      2.1 Loan. The Lender hereby agrees to make the Loan to the Borrower, the proceeds of which shall be disbursed upon the Lender's receipt of all invoices in form and substance satisfactory to the Lender in its sole discretion verifying the use of such proceeds. The proceeds of the Loan shall be used by the Borrower as follows: (a) $229,340 shall be used to purchase equipment in connection with the Business; and (b) $120,660 shall be used to provide permanent working capital in connection with the Business.

2.2 Note; Payment. In order to evidence the Loan and the terms of repayment thereof with interest, the Borrower agrees to execute a Note at the time of the execution of this Agreement, in favor of the Lender, in the original principal amount of $350,000 (as amended, restated, modified, substituted, extended and renewed from time to time, the "**Note**"). All payments under the Loan and all other Obligations shall be repaid in lawful money of the United States which at the time and place of payment is legal tender for the payment of public and private debts.

2.3 Interest. All sums lent to Borrower pursuant to this Agreement shall bear interest at a rate or rates of interest set forth in the Note.

2.4 Loan Fee. Borrower shall pay Lender a loan origination fee to the Lender equal to $7,875.

3. Creation of Security Interest.

3.1 As security for the payment and performance of the Obligations (defined below), the Borrower hereby assigns, pledges and grants to the Lender, and covenants and agrees that the Lender shall have a first priority, perfected and continuing security interest in the Collateral (defined below). The Collateral shall at all times maintained free from any and all security interests, liens, encumbrances, charges, assignments, reservations of title, financing statements, and rights of third parties whatsoever (collectively, "**Liens**") other than Liens in favor of the Lender, Liens, if any, set forth on EXHIBIT A to this Agreement, and Liens approved in advance by the Lender in writing, in its sole and absolute discretion, prior to their creation.

As used in this Agreement, the term:

"**Collateral**" shall mean all of the personal property of the Borrower, all whether now owned or existing or hereafter acquired or created and wherever situated, and shall include, without limitation, the following:

(a) All inventory, and all warranties, licenses, franchises, and general intangibles related thereto (including, without limitation, software) and all returned, rejected or repossessed goods; and

(b) All accounts, contract rights, chattel paper (including, without limitation, electronic chattel paper), instruments, payment intangibles and other general intangibles, health-care-insurance receivables and documents, and all returned, rejected or repossessed goods, the sale or lease of which shall have given or shall give rise to any of the foregoing; and

(c) All equipment, furniture, fixtures, and other goods together with (i) all additions, parts, fittings, accessories, special tools, attachments and accessions now and hereafter affixed thereto and/or used in connection therewith, (ii) leases and chattel paper with respect thereto, (iii) all replacements thereof and substitutions therefore and (iv) and all warranties, licenses, franchises, and general intangibles related to the foregoing (including, without limitation, software); and

(d) All general intangibles, including, without limitation, all books and records, things in action, contractual rights, tax returns, goodwill, literary rights, rights to performance, copyrights, trademarks, patents and commercial tort claims; and

(e) All notes, notes receivable, drafts, letters of credit, letter-of-credit rights, supporting obligations, deposit accounts, investment property, security, acceptances, instruments and documents; and

(f) all insurance policies and insurance proceeds related to any and all of the foregoing or otherwise, all refunds of unearned insurance premiums, and all cash and noncash proceeds thereof, and all books and records in whatever media (paper, electronic or otherwise) recorded or stored, with respect to any or all of the foregoing and all equipment, hardware and general intangibles necessary, beneficial or desirable to retain, access and/or process the information contained in those books and records, and all proceeds (cash and noncash) of the foregoing, it being the intention of the Borrower that the Collateral shall include all of the Borrower's personal property.

"**Loan Documents**" means this Agreement, any and all promissory notes and any and all other documents, instruments, guarantees, certificates, agreements, loan agreements, security agreements, guaranties, deeds of trust, mortgages, assignments or other contract with or for the benefit of the Lender, or securing or evidencing payment of any indebtedness of the Borrower, previously, simultaneously or hereafter executed and/or delivered by the Borrower, any guarantor and/or any other person in connection with any Loan or any of the other Obligations, all as the same may be amended, modified, restated, substituted, extended and renewed at any time and from time to time.

"**Obligations**" means all present and future indebtedness, duties, obligations, and liabilities, whether now existing or contemplated or hereafter arising, of the Borrower to the Lender under, arising pursuant to, in connection with and/or on account of the provisions of this Agreement and/or any of the other Loan Documents or the Loans, including, without limitation, the principal of, and interest on, the Note, late charges, the fees, costs and expenses of any nature whatsoever incurred at any time and from time to time (whether before or after an Event of Default) by the Lender in connection with the negotiation and preparation of this Agreement and each of the Loan Documents, in connection with filing and/or recording taxes or fees, all title insurance premiums and costs, Lien and other record searches, in connection with the administration of the Loans, and in exercising or enforcing any rights, powers and remedies provided in this Agreement or any of the other Loan Documents, including, without limitation, attorney's fees, court costs, receiver's fees, management fees and costs incurred in the repair, maintenance and operation of, or taking possession of, or selling, the Collateral; and also means all other present and future indebtedness, duties, obligations, and liabilities, whether now existing or contemplated or hereafter arising, of the Borrower to the Lender or its affiliates of any nature whatsoever, regardless of whether such indebtedness, duties, obligations, and liabilities be direct, indirect, primary, secondary, joint, several, joint and several, fixed or contingent; and also means any and all renewals, extensions, substitutions, amendments, restatements and rearrangements of any such indebtedness, duties, obligations, and liabilities.

3.2 The Borrower represents and warrants that the Borrower is the absolute owner of the Collateral, holding title to all of the Collateral free and clear of any and all Liens whatsoever except as described below, and the security interest granted to the Lender in this Agreement is and shall at all times constitute a valid, enforceable and perfected first priority security interest and lien on the Collateral, subject to no other Liens other than other security interests in favor of the Lender.

4.   [Borrower Representations and Warranties regarding authority, etc.]

5.   [Borrower Covenants regarding reporting, etc.]

6. [Default.]

7. [Remedies.]

8. [Other Agreements.]

To evidence the parties' agreement to this Agreement they have executed and delivered it on the date stated in the preamble.

GLOBAL PAINT & HARDWARE, Inc.
d/b/a Global Club Hardware

By: _____
    Patricia Bouvier
    President

SECOND BANK OF SPRINGFIELD

By: _____
    Milhause Van Houten
    Senior Vice President

Security Agreement Representations, Warranties and Covenants

Skills: Organization & Risk Allocation
with Drafting Techniques

Covenant Warranty

Overview

THIS EXERCISE continues to refine your drafting technique by exploring how drafters organize the parts of a contract and how they use representations, warranties, covenants to allocate risk between the parties. You will work with a template to improve its organization and negotiate representations, warranties and covenants that reflect the level of risk that the debtor and bank are willing to bear and the parties rights and obligations. Transactional attorneys use a drafting technique called a "qualifier" to specify the level of risk each party bears. Qualifiers can specify a level of risk in at least two ways: on the basis of a party's knowledge and on the basis of materiality.

The two core skills developed here are (1) how to present information logically and (2) how to protect your client's business interests while also accommodating the interests of the other side. Logical organization is a lawyerly topic that you are unlikely to discuss with clients, but the client's business goals are central to the transaction and may require conferring with clients so that you understand what they are paying you to do.

In lending contracts like the one here, the bank generally has two main goals. Its first goal—most likely to actually happen—is for the debtor to pay down its debt as promised. The bank's second goal focuses on events that are less likely to occur, but if they do happen, they get in the way of the first goal. Debtor fraud is high on that list, as well as devaluation or destruction of the collateral through flood, fire, theft or other means. The bank therefore wants representations, warranties and covenants about the debtor paying down the promissory note, and also notice of anything that jeopardizes the bank's likelihood of being able to collect the debt. The debtor also has two goals: first to get money, and second, to make sure that it does not let that goal blind it to the danger of promising more than it can deliver. For example, the debtor will likely have to promise not to transfer any collateral, but will want permission for routine sales of inventory.

Part I explains drafting essentials of organizing, formatting and fine-tuning risk of loss, Part II applies those lessons by having you negotiate representations, warranties, and covenants, Part III brings it all together as you edit the security agreement template to reflect the terms you have agreed to.

Part I: Contract Drafting Essentials Explained

Transactional attorneys write well by logically organizing an agreement's provisions, writing as clearly as possible, and fine-tuning provisions with qualifiers that allocate risk in gradations through qualified representations, warranties, and covenants. This section proceeds from the general to the specific. It starts with the macro—how to organize an agreement's provisions and subparts within each provision—then addresses grammatical and formatting conventions, and finishes with material distinguishing between flat and qualified representations, warranties, and covenants.

A. Getting Organized[1]

Before setting pen to paper, the drafter determines the client's objectives, identifies the audience, masters the legal and factual context in which the document will operate, decides with the client what to include in the document, and chooses or creates the appropriate legal

---

1   Based on Haggard and Kuney *Legal Drafting*, 185–191.

and factual concepts. Those steps give drafters a mass of data and insights that they must assemble into some kind of order. Drafters then make decisions about three ways to organize the document and its subparts: division, classification, and sequence.

1. Division

Division involves creating the hierarchical categories into which the data is to be placed. In the document, divisions will appear in sections that are numbered and have headings. Rational division follows three rules: (1) mutual exclusivity; (2) total coverage; and (3) singularity of principle. To illustrate these rules, assume a division that separates the class of "motor vehicles" into two subclasses, "Ford cars" and "red cars." Consider how that division violates all three rules.

> **Rule One**—*Mutual Exclusivity.* The categories must be mutually exclusive, meaning that no datum can fall into two or more categories. If the categories are mutually exclusive, then a particular provision can go in only one place. Where, however, would you put a red Ford Mustang?

> **Rule Two**—*Total Coverage.* The categories together must equal the entire class; there must be nothing left over. Everything that the drafter wants to put into the document must have a place. But where in the motor vehicles classification scheme suggested above would you place a green Toyota Tundra? The drafter who cannot find a place in the divisional scheme for a particular provision often creates a new category, "miscellaneous," that ends up being full of minor, unrelated, substantive provisions. That is a bad divisional scheme.

> **Rule Three**—*Singularity of Principle.* The division should be based on one consistently applied principle. Red cars and Fords are divisions based on two principles—color and make. This division would totally confuse a user of the document.

Within each category, the drafter should create as many sub-categories as needed—moving from the general down to each specific provision. Each sub-category should also follow the rules of division. For example, within the "cars" category, a drafter might create the following sub-category levels in descending order:

> *III. Cars*
> > *A. Manufacturer*
> > > *1. Make*
> > > > *a. Model*
> > > > > *(1) Year*
> > > > > > *(a) Color*
> > > > > > > *(i) Vehicle Identification Number*

As in that example, the main category and every subcategory should have an appropriate letter or number designation for easy identification and a descriptive heading although that is sometimes omitted at the lowest level of division. While legislative drafters must follow the rules or conventions of statutory drafting, the private law drafter has discretion to have more or fewer sub-categories. But all drafters should also follow rules of outlining.

If a category has sub-categories, it must have at least two. Although often violated, this is not an arbitrary rule. Its logical justification derives from the fact that a category is the sum of its parts. The category heading is simply a more generalized way of expressing what the various parts add up to. A well-organized outline provides information and insight about both individual components, indicating what they represent as a whole, and the whole, indicating what is consists of. In contrast, the following example is a meaningless distinction or division:

> *I. Compensation*
>   *A. Salary*
>
> *II. Etc.*

A better organization would read like this:

> *I. Compensation*
>   *A. Base Salary*
>   *B. Commissions*
>   *C. Bonuses*
>   *D. Stock Options*

If the remuneration under the contract is a salary of $70,000 a year and the employee does not get bonuses, stock options, or other forms of compensation, then it does not make sense to give a broad designation, "compensation," and a more specific designation, "salary." Call it one thing or the other and make it a single category.

Headings should be carefully worded to accurately identify the category's contents. If each provision has been properly classified and put within a particular category, then these provisions will have a common denominator. Determine what it is and word the headimg accordingly. For example, an employee's compensation can include the common denominator of base salary, commissions, and bonuses. Give the category that heading, rather than something unenlightening like "Employee Rights." (A header titled "Employee Rights" also suffers from over-inclusion, since the employee will also have non-compensation rights under the contract.)

A correct description is important for two reasons. First, a reader looking for a particular contract provision will be able to scan the bolded headings and find the relevant provision quickly. If it is buried under a non-descriptive heading, finding it would be difficult and time consuming. Second, the wording of the heading may have legal significance. A court may refuse to enforce a disclaimer of warranties that is contained in a section entitled "SELLER'S WARRANTIES." And a category headed "Employee's Duties," could make it difficult for the employer to later claim that the document created an independent contractor relationship rather than one of employer/employee.

Some state statutes that dictate the form and content of legislation contain a provision stating that "headings are not part of the statute." This provision is designed to prevent the wording of a heading from having any legal significance regarding the interpretation of the statute. Unfortunately, disclaimers of this kind also sometimes appear in private contracts. This clause seems to admit that the drafter is either too lazy to find the proper words to describe a collection of provisions or lacks the linguistic competence to do so.

2. Classification

Classification involves putting each bit of information into its proper category and sub-category. If the drafter of an apartment lease has created a category entitled "Limits on Occupancy," then a specific provision dealing with overnight guests should be included under that heading, not under one dealing with "Alteration of the Premises." Conversely, a provision prohibiting the replacement of ceiling fixtures should not be put in the "Limits on Occupancy" category.

The classification decision is more difficult if the drafter has fudged a bit in complying with the rules of division, especially the one requiring the sub-classes to be mutually exclusive. Indeed, no division can be completely airtight, and some items can usually fit into more than one category. For example, a prohibition against smoking at the worksite could go in an employment policy's "Safety" section or in its "Employee Rules of Conduct" section, depending perhaps on the purpose of the rule. In making classification decisions, the drafter must always keep the user in mind. If a user wanted to find a provision dealing with a specific topic, where would that person look first? The provision should go there.

In practice, division and classification are related intellectual processes. Although a rough divisional scheme usually comes first, the process of classification will often reveal defects and may even suggest an entirely different scheme. Moreover, these division and classification rules reflect the ideal. Sometimes it takes more time than the client is willing to pay for to follow them rigorously, especially when dealing with subsections. After all of the provisions of the document have been classified, the drafter may find an odd one that does not seem to fit anywhere. The drafter should include this provision in whatever section it is most relevant to, rather than completely redo the division scheme and force it to a level of abstraction that is more confusing than useful. Experts in contract drafting prefer that solution to creating a "Miscellaneous" category.

3. Sequence

The sequence of the major components of a contract is discussed in exercise #1: title, preamble, recitals, words of agreement and consideration, substantive provisions (i.e., definitions, representations and warranties, covenants), boilerplate, testimonium, and signature blocks. Within the substantive provisions, and often within a particular clause, drafters must select one of several sequences. The overall document may follow one general sequence, but the major sections may have their own internal logical sequence. Whatever sequence the drafter adopts, the measure of its validity is the extent to which it helps readers use the document in the regulation of their affairs. The major sequential possibilities are as follows:

a. Chronological

If the document will regulate a relationship extending over several phases, then the drafter can deal with the events in the order in which they are going to occur. The sequence of a construction contract, for example, could parallel the construction process itself. Similarly, the major divisions of a lease can be presented in roughly chronological order, as follows:

- *Pre-occupancy:* identity of the parties, identity of the premises, duration, rent, and other fundamentals.

- *Occupancy:* limits on use of the premises, landlord's right to enter for maintenance and repairs, noise abatement, and other matters relevant to when the tenant is in possession.

- *Termination:* condition of the premises, return of security, and other post-occupancy matters.

Your security agreement should reflect this sequence. Start with the substantive provisions that contain crucial language creating the security interest in collateral to secure an obligation, proceed with representations, warranties, and covenants, and end with endgame and boilerplate provisions.

The headings of a chronologically-divided document should indicate that order. Unsophisticated readers, like many of those involved in consumer transactions, can better understand a complex document if it is organized by reference to the sequential actions of the various parties rather than to abstract legal classifications. Thus, rather than referring to "Revocation Rights," which is a legal concept, you could title it "Revoking the Contract," to emphasize the action. Since that provision usually becomes relevant at the end of a contractual relationship, it should appear toward the end of the contract.

b. Importance

Within a category of related rules, a drafter might choose to present the most important ones first. For example, in an employment contract, salary is a central term, while the employee's choice of make and color of company car probably is not. In your security agreement, granting the security interest should likewise appear at the beginning of the substantive provisions. Unscrupulous drafters will sometimes put an extremely important provision that strongly favors their client at the end of a long document, often following or included among a series of trivial provisions. In extreme cases of deception, usually involving consumer transactions, the courts have declined to enforce these provisions.

c. Frequency of Occurrence

Provisions dealing with events that are likely to occur frequently during the transaction can precede those dealing with rare or episodic events. In a construction contract change orders are a frequent occurrence and discovery of historical artifacts is not. In your security agreement, the debtor's duty to make monthly payments on the promissory note should be early on in the debtor's covenants. Less frequent occurrences like changes in name or location of debtor or collateral should appear later in the agreement.

d. Familiar Before Unfamiliar

Some transactions are built around a familiar set of facts or events, with the rights and duties of the parties being fairly commonplace. A particular transaction, however, may move off into previously uncharted territory. To give the parties a shared point of departure, the drafter may choose to deal with the familiar provisions first and then move into the more novel aspects of the undertaking.

e. Rules Before Exceptions

Start with a general rule then specify any exceptions. Exceptions to exceptions, of course, come next. For example, a section of a harbor regulation might contain a long list of things that a vessel under way is required to do. A drafter could follow that enumeration with a list of situations where the general rules do not apply, such as in an emergency. Putting the exceptions before the general rule would only confuse the reader. If the debtor in your security agreement has the right to sell inventory in the ordinary course of business, but also covenants not to transfer the collateral, then the prohibition on transfer should come before the exceptional circumstances of retail sales of collateral that is inventory.

f. What Before How

A description of what the parties to a document must do generally should come before a description of how they are required to do it. For example, a contract for the sale of goods would normally indicate what is being sold, by and to whom, and for how much. It would then cover how delivery and payment are to be made. In your security agreement, the debtor first covenants to notify the lender of damage to collateral, and later agrees to the method of that notice (i.e., first class mail, delivered to the bank's address specified in the preamble).

g. Substance Before Procedure

Regardless of the nature of the document, the substantive provisions should normally come before the procedural or enforcement provisions. For example, an employer's sexual harassment policy would first identify what is being prohibited. Then it would describe the procedures that the employer will follow in enforcing the policy. Likewise, your security agreement should cover procedural issues like how to give notice and dispute resolution provisions that specify choice of law toward the end of the agreement.

We now proceed from this macro level of organizing a contract to the micro level of organizing a sentence.

B. Techniques for Clear Writing[2]

Clarity and consistency should run through a document, from its overall organization to the organization and writing in each provision. This section briefly explains five techniques that tighten writing.

1. Active Voice

The active voice is usually shorter and more direct than the passive voice and thus better for drafted documents. As explained in exercise #2, passive voice increases ambiguity by masking who must do something, or the action to be taken. Consider, for example, what key information is left out of this provision: "Notice must be given within ten days of filing any claim."

2. Present Tense

A contract is said to be constantly speaking - both at the time it is drafted and whenever the parties or a court apply it. Consequently, contracts rarely use past and future tense. A provision should read "if Builder's default is caused by..." instead of "if Builder's default was caused by." Likewise, definitions should read "'Collateral' means... instead of "'Collateral' shall mean..."[3]

Keep in mind, though, that an exception to this rule and the preference for active voice applies to some representations and warranties. Say a car purchase contract contains a representation and warranty about the mileage on the car. Seller may know that the car has been driven

---

2   Based on Haggard, *Contract Law from A Drafting Perspective* 29-31 (2003).

3   As covered in § I(D) below, an additional problem with the future tense for this definition is the use of "shall" for a provision that is not a covenant.

36,000 miles, but does not know who drove the car each of those miles. Accordingly, that representation and warranty could read as follows, "Seller warrants that the Car has been driven 36,000 miles."

3. Ration "to be" Verbs

The "to be" verbs include "was," "is," "are," "were," and "been." Active verbs are usually clearer and more concise. Thus, instead of saying "If Contractor is unable to...," say "If Contractor cannot...". Smoking out "to be" verbs will also enable you to replace passive voice with active voice, since passive voice constructions often include some version of "to be."

4. Avoid Nominalizations

A nominalization is created when the drafter turns a noun into a verb. It makes for long sentences because it requires the addition of another verb to replace the now-nominalized verb to make it grammatical. The simple verb "alter" becomes "an alternation," to which the drafter must now add the verb "make." Nominalizations are wordy and confusing. Go back to the pure verb form of the expression.

> - Replace *have knowledge of* with *know.*
>
> - Replace *submit a payment* with *pay.*
>
> - Replace *make provision for* with *provide.*

5. Avoid Expletives

Resist the temptation to swear in your agreement—though you will be in good company if you swear out loud when you discover yet another typo after printing out the "final" draft. Grammarians use "expletive" in a different sense, to describe phrases like "it is" and "there are." However, the "it" and "there" have no substantive content and are merely noise words inserted to satisfy the syntactical requirements of an English sentence. Expletives are thus wordy and obscure meaning, bad characteristics in a drafted document. Some expletives are so much of our speech pattern that replacing them with other words would make the sentence ponderous and odd-sounding—as in replacing "it is raining" with "the rain is falling down." Often, however, expletives can and should be eliminated, especially when they accompany other drafting- style and usage violations, as in these two examples:

> - Replace *it is the Seller's duty to* with *Seller shall*.
>
> - Replace *there are four exceptions to the Seller's duty to repair* with *the Seller's duty to repair is subject to four exceptions.*

C. Flat and Qualified Representations and Warranties

Recall from exercise #1 that a representation and warranty is a statement of a present or past fact that the other party relies on. A contract clause includes the entire phrase "represents and warrants" to create both a promise that a particular fact is true and to indemnify the other party if it turns out not to be true.

A drafter's job is to allocate risk between the parties. Flat warranties apportion most of the risk to the person making the representation. Lawyers can protect their clients from bearing all of that risk by limiting the representation with what drafters call a "qualifier." The discussion below describes two kinds of qualifiers: knowledge qualifiers and materiality qualifiers.

1. Qualifiers

Qualifiers reduce a party's obligation. Take the sale of a used car with an odometer indicating that it has been driven 36,000 miles. The seller could represent that the car has been driven 36,000 miles, which is a flat warranty. If the car has in fact been driven 50,000 miles but the prior owner set back the odometer, then the seller would be in breach even if she did not know about the prior owner's deceitfulness. So a smart seller would only promise what she knows: that "to the best of her knowledge" the car has been driven 36,000.

The best way to understand the difference between flat and qualified warranties is to trace a clause that starts flat and adds qualifiers. In your security agreement, FNB will want a representation and warranty from the debtor regarding claims outstanding against the collateral to make sure that FNB has top priority in case of default and foreclosure.

FNB might start the negotiation by suggesting this flat representation and warranty:

> *Debtor represents and warrants that there are no claims outstanding against the collateral.*

The debtor's counsel could object that there may be claims to the collateral that the debtor has no knowledge of. A customer may have slipped and fallen in an aisle and be preparing to sue, and the debtor would have no knowledge of the claim. The debtor ought not be in breach if the customer files a suit after FNB and the debtor sign the Security Agreement. Accordingly, debtor's counsel could edit the clause to add a knowledge qualifier, as follows:

> *Debtor represents and warrants that* **to the best of its knowledge** *there are no claims outstanding against the collateral.*

Now consider other kinds of claims that could exist against the collateral, some of which the store could know about yet would not want to bear the risk of those claims causing it to be in default under the security agreement. For example, say that a customer bought a $99 ladder that did not work properly but did not cause personal injury or other big-damage claims. The customer has a claim against the store for a refund or exchange. That claim—probably worth only $99—is for such a small amount of money that its existence should not harm the bank's interests. Accordingly, the debtor's counsel could also propose adding a materiality qualifier to the representation and warranty regarding claims as follows:

> *Debtor represents and warrants that there are no* **material** *claims outstanding against the collateral.*

If you notice that a cautious—or well-represented—debtor would want both knowledge and materiality qualifiers, and that "material" may require a definition such as "claim for more than $1,000," you are getting the gist of drafting. That combination would read as follows:

> *Debtor represents and warrants that* **to the best of its knowledge** *no* **Material** *claims exist against the collateral.*

> *Definitions*
> *"Material"* *means any claim for $1,000 or more, made against the Collateral, by any person other than the Lender.*

Lenders in secured transactions generally prefer a flat warranty on the issue of claims against the collateral because it shifts the risk to the debtor. Debtors, conversely, are better off with qualified representations and warranties regarding claims against the collateral. Negotiations turn on those issues, at least when a debtor has sufficient bargaining power and sophistication to propose a qualified representation and warranty. The hypothetical transaction between Bolt's Urban Hardware and FNB presumes that Bianca Bolt has unusually strong bargaining power in her negotiations with the bank.

D. Covenants: Will and Shall[4]

Recall from exercise #1 that covenants create obligations to do or not do something. Though drafters differ on best practices, the prevailing view is to use the word "shall" only in covenants but not in other provisions of a contract. "Shall" clearly defines an obligation by indicating that one person is obliged to do or not do something, so generally a party's name appears immediately before "shall." For example "Seller shall deliver," and "Borrower shall not transfer the Collateral." If the party fails or refuses, then she is in breach. This construction makes sense because only a party can be the subject of the verb "shall." Thus "Debtor shall notify Lender . . . ." properly expresses a covenant, while "interest shall accrue at a rate of . . ." and "the Closing shall occur on September 1 . . ." are improper ways to use "shall." Interest rates cannot be sued for breach if they fail to accrue, nor can a Closing be sued for failing to happen as expected.

---

4 Based on Haggard, *Contract Law from a Drafting Perspective* 55–56 (2003).

A major goal of a contract is to create certain legal consequences. Despite the importance of unambiguously stating a contract duty, some drafters either use "shall" and "will" interchangeably or prefer one over the other. Many if not most drafters prefer the stronger "shall," since it is a term of command—and also because courts and parties may construe "will" as simply referring to the future. Others think of contracts primarily in terms of promise, rather than command, with "will" more accurately reflecting this promissory effect. You should adopt one convention or another and adhere to it throughout the contract.

For example

> *Seller shall [or will] deliver the goods within 10 days after the date of this contract.*

Duties to refrain from acting are created with the words "shall not" or "will not." Negations of, exceptions to, and qualifications upon previously created duties are expressed by saying "is not required to." Options, which transactional attorneys call "discretionary authority," are expressed with "may."

For example

> *Seller shall deliver the goods by within 10 days after the date of this contract.* ***Seller is not required to provide notice of the exact day of delivery.***

Because the term "shall" gets used and misused in so many different ways it's helpful to see some errors and how they should be fixed. Here is a list with edits showing the improvements.

> Seller may ~~shall have the right to~~ inspect the goods prior to delivery. Seller shall ~~have the duty to~~ arrange for shipment within 10 days.
>
> Buyer's power of acceptance ~~shall~~ expires in 30 days after . . . . the contract is ~~shall be~~ subject to the laws of the State of Texas.

Because of the endemic misuse of "shall" and "will," some drafters have abandoned both terms and use "must" and "must not" to create duties to act or refrain from acting. This usage, however, deprives the drafter of an effective word for creating conditions, and "must" cannot be used for both purposes. This text adheres to the "shall" convention and reserves "must" for creating conditions. We discuss conditions in detail in exercise #6 on endgame provisions.

Problem 5: Flat and Qualified Representations, Warranties and Covenants

For each of the following clauses identify (1) whether it's a representation and warranty or a covenant (or both); and (2) whether it's flat or qualified either by knowledge or materiality. Also correct any improper uses of "shall" or other drafting errors.

   a. Debtor represents and warrants that there are no claims outstanding against the Collateral.

   b. Debtor represents and warrants that no claims exist against it, nor shall they.

   c. Debtor will keep the Collateral in good order and repair at all times and shall immediately notify the Secured Party of any event causing a material loss or decline in value of the Collateral.

   d. Seller shall inspect the Goods prior to delivery and notify Buyer of all defects that it discovers.

Part II: Negotiation

Before you start to negotiate the representations, warranties and covenants, sit down and make a list of what your client wants to protect and what it wants to avoid. Start by making a list of things that can go wrong from both parties' perspective, from small matters like a payment lost in the mail to more serious events like the debtor transferring the collateral for fraudulent purposes.

Also, what is the most important representation and warranty that bank will want the debtor to make? What are the qualifiers that the debtor will want? What arguments can the debtor make to justify those materiality or knowledge qualifiers?

Once you have your list, identify the contract concepts that will protect your client. For example, the debtor may want a qualifier of its covenant not to transfer its property without FNB's prior written consent so that the store can sell inventory. FNB for its part could want representations, warranties and covenants regarding the debtor's compliance with laws such as fair employment practices and licensing requirements to operate the store.

Negotiate with the lawyer representing the other side. If your professor provides handouts that convey instructions from your client, comply with professional obligations regarding confidentiality. Do not tell the student who represents the other party what your client told you except as necessary to follow the client's instructions.

Part III: Student Assignment Representations, Warranties, and Covenants

Now you are ready to apply these rules of organization and wordsmithing to memorialize the agreement.

The sample security agreement below is the same one used in exercises #2 and #4. Review its organization and consider how to improve it. Make a list of representations, warranties and covenants in the template and decide how to organize them in your agreement. As always, edit out legalese, write in the active voice, and otherwise seek to write precisely, clearly, and consistently.

A. Tips for the Exercise

Organization

- Consider whether to organize the sections by contract concept (representations and warranties, covenants, etc.), or by business concerns like issues regarding the collateral and other issues like borrower being authorized to operate a hardware store.

- Consider how to tabulate to make the provisions easier to read.

- Use headings to describe each provision.

Substance

- Remember that a representation is a statement of a present or past fact, while a warranty shifts liability to the warrantor if the fact proves not to be true. Accordingly, the two terms almost always occur in tandem, as in "Borrower represents and warrants that . . ."

- Using "shall" and the active voice will clarify precisely who has to do what to whom. If you qualify an obligation—i.e., require that Borrower provide notice of any "material" theft, fire, or other loss of collateral—you lessen the risk borne by the debtor.

• Skills: Organization & Risk Allocation with Drafting Techniques

- Remember that representations, warranties and covenants function in tandem with provisions that you will work with in exercise #6 regarding the events that justify a lender in declaring default and the consequences of that default.

B. Checklist for Organization, Qualifiers and Language

General

❑ Accurately embodies negotiated terms

❑ Covers all relevant facts

❑ All parts of the agreement work together

❑ Defined terms are consistently, appropriately used

❑ Cross-references are easy to follow and not too abundant

❑ Reads like good prose; clear, concise, smooth, well organized

❑ Reader ends up knowing all of the rights and duties of the parties

❑ Reader ends up with all significant questions answered

❑ Reader can understand the terms of the deal

Representations, Warranties and Covenants

❏ Review flat and qualified representations, warranties and covenants for accuracy

❏ Use "shall" with covenants but not other provisions

Review Each Part to Avoid These Language Issues

❏ Improper use of "Shall"

❏ Legalese

❏ Wordiness

❏ Passive voice

❏ Inconsistency

❏ Ambiguity

❏ Omission of articles (i.e., a, an, the)

❏ Incorrect verb tenses

❏ Nominalizations instead of strong verbs

❏ Double negatives

❏ Dangling modifiers

❏ Sentence fragments

❏ Run-on sentences

Proofread Carefully to Avoid these Errors

- ❏ Missing words

- ❏ Extra words

- ❏ Missing word endings

- ❏ Spell check errors

- ❏ Commas in the wrong place

- ❏ Colons and Semicolons used incorrectly

- ❏ Periods missing

- ❏ Tabulations punctuated improperly

C. Template

Download the template from the book website and edit it to make the document work for the transaction between Bolt's Urban Hardware and FNB. Cut and paste the front matter, end matter, and basic terms from exercises #2 and #4 into the security agreement below. Because this exercise involves representations, warranties, and covenants, the provisions that are not part of this assignment are deleted, leaving only the headers surrounded by brackets (i.e., "[default]"). Use the track changes function of your word processing system then create a separate document that incorporates the changes without showing the edits.

Pass in the clean copy and retain the copy with tracked changes for your records.

LOAN AND SECURITY AGREEMENT

THIS LOAN AND SECURITY AGREEMENT (this "Agreement") is made this 12th day of June, 2017, by and between SECOND BANK OF SPRINGFIELD (the "Lender"), with a mailing address for the purposes of this Agreement at 123 Fake St., Springfield, NY 13333, Attn: Milhause Van Houten, and GLOBAL PAINT & HARDWARE, Inc. (d/b/a Global Club Hardware), a New York corporation (the "Borrower"), with a chief executive office and mailing address for the purposes of this Agreement of 747 Hammer Dr., Shelbyville, NY 13332.

RECITALS

A. The Borrower is engaged in the business of operating a Club Hardware store (the "Business") at the following location: 747 Hammer Dr., Shelbyville, NY 13332 (the "Business Premises").

B. The Borrower has applied to the Lender for a term loan in the original principal amount of $350,000 (the "Term Loan," and all other extensions of credit by the Lender to the Borrower being sometimes hereinafter referred to collectively as the "Loans").

C. The Lender is willing to provide the Loans on the condition that the Borrower enters into this Agreement, which shall, among other things, govern and secure the Loans.

NOW, THEREFORE, in consideration of the foregoing and of the mutual promises, covenants and agreements of the parties contained in this Agreement, the parties do agree as follows:

1. [Interpretation.]

2. [The Loans.]

3. [Creation of Security Interest.]

4. [Promises Regarding the Collateral]

    4.1 The Lender (or any person designated by the Lender) shall have the right at any reasonable time to enter the Borrower's premises and examine, audit, and inspect the Collateral and all books and records pertaining to the Collateral and the Borrower shall assist the Lender in whatever way necessary to make any inspection.

4.2 The Borrower shall deliver to the Lender originals of all of the Borrower's letters of credit, investment property, chattel paper, documents and instruments and the Borrower shall execute and deliver all such separate pledges, assignments, and security interests with regards to such items of Collateral in form and substance acceptable to the Lender.

4.3 The Borrower represents and warrants that the Borrower is the absolute owner of the Collateral, holding title to all of the Collateral free and clear of any and all Liens whatsoever except as described below, and the security interest granted to the Lender in this Agreement is and shall at all times constitute a valid, enforceable and perfected first priority security interest and lien on the Collateral, subject to no other Liens other than other security interests in favor of the Lender.

4.4 Collateral will be kept in good condition and in a good state of repair and will not be wasted, destroyed, misused or allowed to deteriorate, ordinary wear and tear excepted.

4.5 Collateral will be kept only at the Borrower's business located on the Business Premises.

4.6 The Borrower, as the Lender may request and require from time to time, shall procure, execute and deliver to the Lender any security agreement, financing statements, releases, lien waivers or other writing or record that the Lender deems necessary or beneficial to create, perfect (by filing, control, and/or otherwise), preserve, continue, protect or enforce the Lender's rights and interests under this Agreement, under the other Loan Documents and the Lender's first priority and only Lien in and to the Collateral (including, without limitation, the first priority of record of the Lender's Liens in the Collateral), or in any other security for the Obligations. The Borrower shall pay on demand all costs, fees and expenses incurred by the Lender in connection with the taking, perfection, preservation, protection and/or release of a lien on the Collateral. The Borrower hereby authorizes the Lender to file with such applicable state and local filing offices such financing statements and amendments thereto as the Lender shall deem necessary in the Lender's discretion to perfect, and to maintain and continue the perfection of, the security interests granted hereunder.

4.7 The Borrower shall at all times keep the Collateral and the proceeds from any disposition identifiable and separate from the property of any third person.

4.8 The Obligations shall be further secured by the unlimited, continuing guaranty of payment, in form and substance satisfactory to the Lender, of Patricia Bouvier (the "Guarantor").

9. Additional Representations and Warranties. The Borrower represents and warrants to the Lender on the date of this Agreement, and shall be deemed to represent and warrant to the Lender at the time each request for an advance under the Loans is submitted and again at the time any advance is made under the Loans, as follows:

9.1 The Borrower has full power and authority to execute and deliver the Loan Documents and to incur and perform the obligations provided for therein, all of which have been duly authorized by all proper and necessary action of the appropriate governing body of the Borrower. No consent or approval of any governmental authority or other third party is required as a condition to the validity of this Agreement or any of the Loan Documents.

9.2 The Borrower is in compliance with all terms, conditions, covenants and agreements under this Agreement and under the other Loan Documents.

9.3 There is no charter, partnership agreement, operating agreement or other document pertaining to the organization, power or authority of the Borrower, no provision of any existing agreement, mortgage, indenture or contract binding on the Borrower or affecting its property that would conflict with or in any way prevent the execution, delivery or carrying out of the terms of this Agreement and/or any of the other Loan Documents.

9.4 There are no laws, ordinances, statutes, rules, regulations, orders, injunctions, rule of common law, judicial interpretation, writs, or decrees of any federal, state or other political subdivision thereof and any entity exercising executive, legislative, judicial, regulatory or administrative functions of or pertaining to government and any department, agency or instrumentality thereof (all of the foregoing, "Laws") that would conflict with or in any way prevent the execution, delivery or carrying out of the terms of this Agreement and/or any of the other Loan Documents.

9.5 There is no proceeding involving the Borrower pending or, to the knowledge of the Borrower, threatened before any court or governmental authority, agency, instrumentality or arbitration authority.

9.6 The information supplied and statements made by the Borrower, and by each other obligor under any of the Loan Documents, in any financial, credit or accounting statement or application for credit is true and correct in all material respects and is not incomplete by the omission of any material fact necessary to make such information not misleading.

10. Covenants.

10.1 The Borrower will furnish the Lender from time to time such information regarding the business affairs and financial condition of the Borrower and each other obligor under the Loan Documents as the Lender may request, including, but not limited to, periodic balance sheets, income statements and statements of cash flow concerning the Borrower, and copies of the Borrower's federal income tax returns. Without in any way limiting the foregoing, the Borrower shall (1) as soon as available, but in any event, not later than one hundred eighty (180) days after the end of each fiscal year while any of the Obligations remain outstanding, a balance sheet, income statement and statement of cash flow prepared in accordance with United States generally accepted accounting principles, such financial statements to be prepared by the Borrower's certified public account who shall be reasonably satisfactory to the Lender, (2) cause to be provided to the Lender, as soon as available, but in any event, not later than one hundred eighty (180) days after the end of each calendar year while any of the Obligations remain outstanding, the personal financial statements of the Guarantor prepared in accordance with United States generally accepted accounting principles, such financial statements to be prepared by the Guarantor's respective certified public accounts who shall be reasonably satisfactory to the Lender, (3) such other periodic financial statements as the Lender may request, (4) certificates satisfactory to the Lender from responsible officers to the effect that the applicable financial statements are true and correct and fairly reflect the financial position, results of operations and cash flow of the Borrower as of the date of the financial statements and to the further effect that no material adverse change has occurred to the Borrower, its business or financial condition or in the Lender's rights and remedies with respect to, or the value of, the Collateral since such date and that there existed on such date, and there exists on the date of the delivery of the certificate, no Event of Default; and (5) as soon as available, but in any event, not later than thirty (30) days after the due date therefor (including lawful extensions), a complete copy of Borrower's and the Guarantor's federal income tax returns for each tax year of the Borrower and the Guarantor. All financial statements delivered hereunder shall be prepared on the basis of generally accepted accounting principles applied on a consistent basis.

10.2 The Borrower shall maintain its organizational existence in good standing.

10.3 The Borrower shall pay and discharge all taxes, assessments and governmental charges or levies imposed upon it or any of its income or properties prior to the date on which penalties attach thereto, and all lawful claims which, if unpaid, might become a Lien upon any of its properties; provided, however, the Borrower shall not be required to pay any such tax, assessment, charge, levy or claim, the payment of which the Lender is satisfied the Borrower will have the ability to pay without difficulty, the priority and enforcement of any Lien associated therewith is subordinate to the Lender's security interest and is stayed, and the payment of which is being contested in good faith and by proper proceedings.

10.4 The Borrower shall furnish such information as the Lender may from time to time request, and permit or cause to permit the duly authorized representatives of the Lender at all reasonable times to examine the books and records of the Borrower, and take memoranda and extracts therefrom.

10.5 The Borrower shall comply with all Laws to which the Borrower and/or the Collateral are subject.

10.6 The Borrower shall establish and maintain its primary deposit accounts with the Lender, provided that a cash deposit account for daily cash deposits at a banking institution other than the Lender may be deemed acceptable to the Lender at its sole discretion.

10.7 The Borrower agrees to promptly notify the Lender of: (i) any condition or event that constitutes, or with the running of time and/or the giving of notice would constitute, a default under any of the Loan Documents, and any material adverse change in the financial condition of the business of the Borrower or in the Lender's rights and remedies with respect to, or the value of, the Collateral; (ii) any notice, claim or demand from any governmental agency that alleges that the Borrower is in violation of any of the terms of, or has failed to comply with any applicable order issued pursuant to any Laws including, but not limited to, the Occupational Safety and Health Act, the Environmental Protection Act, and the Employee Retirement Income Security Act of 1974; and (iii) with a full description, all litigation and of all proceedings before any court or any governmental or regulatory agency affecting the Borrower which, if adversely decided, would materially affect the conduct of the Borrower's business, the financial condition of the Borrower or in the Lender's rights and remedies with respect to, or the value of, the Collateral.

10.8 The Borrower will maintain insurance with responsible insurance companies on such of its properties, in such amounts and against such risks as is customarily maintained by similar businesses operating in the same vicinity. The Borrower will, at the Borrower's expense, maintain insurance on all Collateral against such risks and in such amounts as the Lender may from time to time require. The foregoing insurance coverage shall at least include, but shall not necessarily be limited to: (i) liability coverage in an amount no less than $1,000,000.00 and property damage coverage of not less than $500,000 or such other amount otherwise acceptable to the Lender in its sole and absolute discretion; and (ii) worker's compensation coverage in such amounts as is required by law; and (iii) business interruption insurance in such coverage amounts as is acceptable to the Lender. If the Borrower fails to provide the required insurance and/or the evidence thereof, the Lender may, in addition to its other rights and remedies, effect such insurance (but shall be under no obligation to do so), and in that event, the Borrower will pay to the Lender, on demand, the full amount of the premiums paid or incurred by the Lender. The Borrower shall provide the Lender with Certificates of Insurance (on ACORD Forms 25 and 28, as applicable), evidencing the insurance coverages required above, with the Lender to be named as Loss Payee with respect to Borrower's casualty insurance, and as additional insured with respect to Borrower's liability insurance. Such insurance certificates shall provide the Lender with at least thirty (30) days' unconditional notice of cancellation of the policies referenced by such certificates.

10.9 The Borrower shall not (i) transfer, create or permit to be acquired any interest in or against the Collateral or the Borrower's other assets, or (ii) permit any Liens, including, without limitation, those with respect to taxes, to remain unpaid to or by any third person without first obtaining the written consent of the Lender, or (iii) engage in any business other than the Business, or (iv) acquire or own any subsidiaries, or (v) incur any indebtedness for borrowed money, except the Obligations, or incur any liabilities except in the ordinary course of business, or (vi) purchase, redeem or otherwise acquire any of its equity interests now or hereafter outstanding, declare or pay any dividends or distribution thereon, apply any of its property or assets to the purchase, redemption or other retirement of, set apart any sum for the payment of any dividends or distributions on, or for the purchase, redemption, or other retirement of, make any distribution by reduction of capital or otherwise in respect of, any shares of any class of equity interests of the Borrower, (vii) make any loan, advance or extension of credit to any individual, partnership, corporation or other entity, other than trade credit on reasonable terms extended to customers of the Borrower in the ordinary course of business, or (viii) engage in any transaction with any person who owns or controls (or who is related to any person who owns or controls) any interest in the Borrower, except reasonable payments for goods and services actually provided in the ordinary course of business on arm's length terms, or (ix) merge, consolidate, transfer all or substantially all of its assets, liquidate, enter into a share exchange, or otherwise alter its capital structure in any manner whatsoever, (x) admit new equity holders, or (xi) permit all or any portion of its equity interests of any class to be transferred. Notwithstanding the foregoing, prior to an Event of Default, Borrower may sell its inventory in the ordinary course of business, and may replace worn out and obsolete equipment provided that such replacement equipment is of equal or greater value than the equipment replaced and is subject to a first priority, perfected security interest in favor of the Lender.

11. [Default.]

12. [Remedies.]

13. [Other Agreements.]

IN WITNESS WHEREOF, the parties hereto have caused this Agreement to be executed under seal and delivered as of the day and year first above written.

> GLOBAL PAINT & HARDWARE, Inc.
> d/b/a Global Club Hardware
> By: _____
> Patricia Bouvier
> President
>
> SECOND BANK OF SPRINGFIELD
> By: _____
> Milhause Van Houten
> Senior Vice President

Security Agreement Endgame Provisions
Skill: Anticipate, Allocate & Minimize Risk

Overview

ENDGAME PROVISIONS appear at the end of a contract and usually become relevant only at the end of a contractual relationship. Accordingly, we tackle these important provisions as the last security agreement exercise in this book.

Recall from your Contracts class that a plaintiff asserting a claim for breach of contract must prove three things: formation, breach, and damages. The exercises in this book are sequenced to mirror those elements. Exercise #4 ensured contract formation by making the security interest attach to the collateral. Then exercise #5 identified representations, warranties, and covenants that defined adequate performance and therefore breach. Third and finally, this exercise precisely identifies what counts as breach—known as "default" in security agreements—and spells out its consequences. Perhaps most important and likely unique to the secured transactions context, this exercise identifies the way that a secured party can use self-help to liquidate the collateral to satisfy the debt. While exercise #4 required that you understand and apply UCC §§ 9–102, 9–203, and 9–108 for the security interest to attach, this exercise demands a deeper engagement in both statutory and drafting rules.

Part 6 of Article 9 allows the parties to change some of their duties regarding default and foreclosure and makes some of the duties fixed, or as contracts scholars phrase it, "immutable." (Contracts scholars describe rules that the parties can contract around as "default rules.") By the end of this exercise you will better understand how to work with default rules such as UCC § 9–612's presumption that 10 days is commercially reasonable notice for collateral disposition, § 9–603's "manifestly unreasonable" standard for contractual definitions of a commercially reasonable disposition, and § 9–624's limits on when a debtor can waive some of its Part 6 rights. Perhaps the exercise's most challenging aspect is the interplay of statutory and common law, reflected in the provisions just noted as well as Article 9's failure to define default. If a drafter does not define default in the security agreement the common law rule applies and only failure to pay constitutes a default. Event of default clauses add events that justify the lender in declaring default, such as debtor transferring collateral or letting insurance coverage lapse.

This mix of common law and statutory elements in a security agreement's endgame provisions calls on all three essential drafting skills: understanding the business deal, translating that into contract concepts, and committing the agreed-upon terms to properly formatted words on the page or screen. We begin with general considerations then zoom in on their application to secured transactions. Part I explains how endgame provisions function as components of contracts generally, then explains the drafter's tool of conditions. Part II applies these lessons to secured transactions, explaining events of default and its consequences so that you can think through common occurrences in a hardware retail business that could prevent the debtor from paying down the loan (or increase the risk of non-payment). Part III then recaps the relevant legal rules. Part IV brings it all together by having you negotiate and draft clauses re: events of default and the consequences that flow from default.

Part I: Endgame Clauses Explained

Before you start to draft, it is helpful to understand a transactional attorney's job of thinking ahead about the positive and negative ways that a relationship can end, an ending's consequences, and the role of conditions in shaping what counts as an ending.

A. Many Types of Endings

All relationships end. They may end on a certain date, when specified events occur, when a party breaches, if an Act of God interferes with the parties' best laid plans, or when the deal's purpose is fulfilled. Even when parties expect a relationship to last forever, a crucial part of your role as an attorney is to help clients plan for both expected and unexpected or acrimonious endings.

Deal-endings fit into three categories: (1) "happy endings," when the deal ends just as the parties planned for it to end; (2) "no-fault endings," those endings that are not the fault of either party, but instead caused by unforeseen, serious events that make performance impossible; and (3) "unhappy endings" that are caused by a party's wrongdoing and produce losses, and perhaps also loathing and litigation. Plan for all three types of endings. Although security agreements focus on unhappy endings, this chapter explains all three types.

As discussed in exercise #5, you should put all of the ending-related clauses at the end of the agreement. Generally speaking, they fit best after the substantive provisions that establish the parameters for the relationship and right before the final interpretive clauses that cover issues like waiver, modification, and merger.[42] Within these ending-related clauses, happy endings generally come first because they relate to the parties' expectations for the deal. The no-fault endings come next. Last of all are the unhappy endings because fighting with each other is the least intended of endings.

1. Happy Endings: Termination & Renewal Clauses

Every deal must establish how it would end if all goes well, which is drafted as a "termination" clause. It occurs in nearly every agreement and specifies when the legal rights and duties in the agreement no

---

42 Merger clauses, also known as integration clauses, reflect the parties' intent that the writing represents the entire statement of their agreement, superseding earlier negotiations and other extrinsic evidence.

longer govern the parties. Termination takes various forms. For example, termination can occur on a specific date. For example:

> *This Agreement terminates on June 25, 2022.*

Or termination can be calculated as a period of time after a specific event:

> *This Agreement terminates six months after the last unit has been sold.*

Or

> *This Agreement terminates two years after the Effective Date.*

Termination can also occur when an event occurs (or fails to occur), as in:

> *This Agreement terminates on the date when Publisher has sold 10,000 copies of the Book.*

Finally, choice is a common way to terminate a deal, whether unilateral or mutual. For example:

> *Either party may terminate this agreement with 10 days prior notice to the other party.*

Some contracts renew on their termination date, either indefinitely or for a certain number of renewal cycles. Renewal is not used in all deals, but is common in intellectual property (IP) deals, licenses, franchises, and leases. If your deal includes a renewal clause, make sure you address the frequency of these renewal cycles, whether any conditions govern renewal, and whether renewal is with any modifications to the original agreement.

2. No-Fault Endings: Force Majeure Clauses

Bad things happen. People get sick or die; tornadoes or fires might destroy the hardware store; changes in the law could make performance virtually impossible; events on the far side of the globe may cause disastrous delays in the supply chain. These unforeseen, severe events that make performance impossible or impracticable are called "force majeure events" (sometimes called "Acts of God"). When a force majeure event occurs, neither the party whose performance is blocked by the event (called the "non-performing party") nor the other party must perform during the force majeure event. Force majeure events create a strange legal limbo in which neither party is liable for breach despite its non-performance, and the agreement continues in force despite performance being suspended. When the force majeure event ends, performance resumes, but if the force majeure event lasts a long time, the parties can terminate the agreement without penalty.

3. Unhappy Endings: Breach, Dispute Resolution and Indemnification

Sometimes parties fail to do what they promised to do. Given that agreements generally depend on trusting that each party will abide by its promises, parties often balk at planning for these very promises to be broken or at negotiating for what remedies should apply to future bad faith actions by either party. Nevertheless, every agreement should include a breach clause (in secured transactions, known as a "default" clause) that addresses three issues: (1) what events constitute an "event of default" or breach; (2) whether the breaching party has a right to cure the breach; and (3) the remedies that are available to the aggrieved party.

Even an impeccably drafted endgame provision will not cover every injury or disagreement. Parties may dispute the scope of their rights or duties, whether a party has in fact breached, or how to interpret the terms of their agreement. So contracts often include a dispute resolution clause that establishes at the very least the procedures for resolving any dispute (litigation or arbitration), the governing law, and the choice of forum.

In some deals, one party is at risk for being sued by third parties with regard to some aspect of this deal. These risks are particularly frequent in IP deals, licenses, and the purchase of existing businesses. Whenever your deal includes the possibility of Party A being sued by a third party for the actions of Party B, you must consider negotiating and drafting an indemnification clause requiring Party B to indemnify Party A for those specific liabilities.

B. Post-Termination Provisions

Even though the agreement has terminated, the parties may continue to have some obligations to each other. Consider whether there will be any tangible objects, intangible rights, assets or debts that were a part of the deal and that might exist when the deal ends. The most common continuing duties relate to confidentiality and non-competition. In addition, some deals may include the right to continue using IP or selling inventory post-termination. In those cases parties generally agree to a corresponding duty to pay royalties or fees on post-termination sales. Make sure you specify the term for any of these continuing duties, as well as any conditions.

Along with continuing duties, there may be one-time close-out duties related to termination. These duties tend to focus on returning the parties to some type of status quo ante such as: returning objects, buildings, or IP rights to the party who previously owned them; destroying documents or records, especially if they contain the other party's confidential information; paying any outstanding deal-related debts; paying a termination fee; terminating the deal's official existence, such as dissolving a company, notifying government agencies, or rescinding any pending filings; and terminating employees. Most clauses related to close-out duties specify deadlines for each duty, and they often include a duty to notify the other party that the close-out duty has been completed.

C. Conditions as a Format for Default Clauses

Recall from exercise #1 that a condition often occurs in an "if ... then ... " sentence structure. Probably the most important condition in security agreements addresses the parties' rights and duties if the debtor breaches the agreement by, for example, failing to make a payment or selling the collateral without telling the secured party. Your job is to plan for that negative endgame to the contract, in good part because most parties hope the transaction will not fall apart, and thus prefer to avoid planning for the unpleasant possibilities.

Drafters use conditions to identify events that trigger default and also the remedies that secured parties can exercise after default. Many or most contracts have remedial provisions even though a court could determine what constitutes breach and shape a remedy. Many clients realize that it is cheaper and simpler to define ahead of time what counts as breach and what consequences follow from it.

Remedial provisions in a security agreement do two things. First, they describe the events that constitute breach. Second, the remedy clauses specify the remedies for breach. As with the other parts of a contract,

• Skill: Anticipate, Allocate & Minimize Risk

the triggering events and remedies vary greatly based on the type of agreement and are often tailored to the specifics of a transaction.

Part II: Endgame in Security Agreements

A. Triggering Events

A primary goal of a remedy provision is to specify with precision what counts as a party's failure to perform its contractual obligations. Consider the secured transaction we have been working on. A core purpose of the contract is to provide the bank with an interest in the debtor's equipment so that the bank can sell the collateral to satisfy at least part of the debt if the debtor defaults. If the debtor sells off that equipment before default, then the bank is left with less collateral to satisfy the debt. Thus the bank here will want to have the right to terminate the contract—aka "declare a default" in the language of secured transaction—if the debtor sells a delivery truck without telling the bank.

Drafters call the clause that lists triggering events an "event of default" clause. Note that this clause is a specialized type of definition. Like other definitions, it groups a number of items under a single phrase, "Events of Default." However, the list of events that constitute an event of default is usually considerably longer than the list of collateral that is defined as "Collateral" earlier in the security agreement. Moreover, one or more of these events counts as an event of default. Accordingly, drafters often format the definition at the beginning or end of the clause with a parenthetical phrase ("each, an **Event of Default**").

Default is a broader concept than breach of contract. Although the listed events of default in a security agreement generally include events that would be a breach of the contract under the common law (for example, non-payment), they can also include many things that would otherwise not be considered a breach, such as the debtor's changed financial status and failure to maintain insurance on collateral. Drafters call these "insecurity" provisions. Default under one contract can also be a default under another agreement, even if the two transactions are entirely separate, with different parties. This provision is known as a "cross-default" clause.

Some events of default are outside of the parties' control. For example, the template security agreement that you will edit includes an insecurity clause that gives the creditor the power to declare default if the debtor "suffers . . . a material adverse change in [its] financial condition." If a big-box store moves in down the street from Bolt's Urban Hardware, it could cause the debtor's default by "materially" reducing the hardware store's income. Debtor's counsel could limit this risk by including a definition of "material" impact on the business. For example, "material" could be defined as more than 10% of the hardware store's net income, averaged over the past three years.

Other examples of default include:

- Failure to pay any amounts when due

- Debtor's false or misleading representations

- Failure to perform any covenant

- Debtor or a guarantor becomes insolvent

- Merger with another company

- Judgments or orders entered against the debtor

- Debtor's default under another agreement

• Skill: Anticipate, Allocate & Minimize Risk

Note that timing is key. A debtor defaults if a representation was false at the time the debtor made it, not if changed circumstances occurring after the date a representation make it no longer true. A representation is merely a statement of present or past fact. Note also that like the change in financial circumstances noted above, a debtor will want to qualify an event of default based on falseness of a representation with a materiality qualifier. For example, the debtor would be in default only if a representation was untrue "in any material respect" when the debtor made it. This materiality qualifier is less likely to be further defined than the money amount discussed in the materiality qualifier about reductions in business, but nevertheless protects the debtor against a hair-trigger default.

Similarly, the debtor's breach of a covenant generally constitutes an event of default. Debtors enjoy grace periods—known as "cure"—for some breached covenants, such as failure to comply with routine reporting requirements that may be mere oversights. In that case the breach would constitute an event of default only if it remains uncured for a specified number of days. The cure period gives the debtor an opportunity to fix the problem that gave rise to the breach. A debtor-friendly cure period commences only after the debtor has knowledge of the breach.

Drafters either draft a separate provision addressing the right to cure or build the cure right into each event of default provision. When some events of default are more serious than others, the latter approach makes more sense.

Banks tend to be unwilling to allow a debtor to cure a serious default such as making fraudulent statements regarding financial matters. Missed payments fall somewhere between these two categories. A missed payment could either be due to a technical glitch like a faulty address or wire transfer, or it could be an early sign that the debtor's business is failing, making a secured creditor eager to swoop in while the collateral still has a high value. Some security agreements balance

these considerations by making it an event of default for the debtor
to miss two consecutive payments, or to miss one payment and fail to
cure it within a set period such as ten business days.

Secured parties can make the occurrence of an event of default
automatically put the debtor in default. In the alternative, the event of
default clause can give the secured party discretionary authority to
declare default or not as it sees fit. The clause could also require the
secured party to notify the debtor that the event of default has occurred
before it declares a default.

B. Consequences of Default

Remedial provisions generally follow the part of a contract that defines
events of default. While some security agreements merely state the
lender's rights under UCC Article 9, a well-drafted contract spells out
exactly what will happen if a covenant is breached. Then a secured
creditor reduces the risk of an expensive and unpredictable dispute
about whether it exceeded its rights in repossessing and foreclosing
on the collateral. As discussed below, UCC §§9–602 and 9–603 shape
these provisions by making some rights immutable—such as a creditor's duty not to breach the peace during repossession—and allowing
contractual definitions of other issues, such as what constitutes a
commercially reasonable disposition of collateral.

A security agreement generally articulates three main consequences
of default: terminating the creditor's duty to provide any more funds,
accelerating the debt, and providing how the creditor can repossess and
dispose of that collateral to satisfy the debt. We address each in turn.

1. Termination

Most contracts give one or both parties the power to terminate the
contract when the other breaches. Sometimes the contract further

provides the non-breaching party with additional remedies, such as the option to collect liquidated damages from the breaching party. Security agreements, which are generally drafted by the secured creditor, often provide that when a debtor is in default—i.e., when it has missed payments—that default terminates the lender's obligation to loan the debtor any additional funds. Many debtors rely on a regular stream of funds from their secured creditor under an arrangement known as a line of credit, in which debtors borrow money as they need it and make periodic payments. Bolt's Urban Hardware, for example, could have borrowed its funds as a line of credit and paid back the bank with a percentage of its daily or weekly cash register receipts. In that situation, the store might not be able to operate without that continued injection of capital to buy inventory, pay its employees, and meet other essential obligations to third parties.

2. Acceleration

Acceleration is the second major remedy in security agreements. It only applies to loans that are paid over time. The line of credit just described could be paid over time, with the debtor obliged to keep it below a set amount such as 50% of the wholesale value of the store's inventory. A simpler example is a financed car purchase, which many students have personal experience with. Say that you borrow $20,000 to pur-chase a car, promise to pay 5% interest and make monthly payments of $600 for three years, and grant the creditor a security interest in the car to secure that obligation. If you miss one payment, then only the $600 would be due. You would be in default, and the secured creditor could repossess the car, but it could only collect $600 from selling the car, because without an acceleration clause you are only in default for the amount of that missed payment. Now assume that the security agreement includes an acceleration clause, as most do. That clause, properly exercised, makes the entire indebtedness immediately due, even though you have only missed one payment.

Like termination of further advances under a line of credit, acceleration may well put a debtor out of business. Just as you would have difficulty writing a $19,400 check in this car purchase example, few debtors have the cash to repay an accelerated debt because they planned to pay gradually over time. Moreover, defaults and accelerations may trigger default under the debtor's other loan agreements via cross-default provisions. Often, the right to accelerate is just as powerful as actually accelerating, because a secured creditor's mere threat to accelerate can get the debtor to make significant concessions that give the creditor the reassurances that it seeks.

Acceleration clauses can be automatic or optional. An automatic acceleration clause provides that the debtor is in default as soon as an event of default occurs, such as a missed payment. Optional acceleration clauses, in contrast, use a phrase like "in Lender's sole discretion" to give the secured party the right to declare default if an event of default happens.

An automatic acceleration clause could read as follows:

> *Upon an Event of Default, Borrower's Obligation becomes immediately due and payable without any further action of any kind.*

An optional acceleration clause, in contrast, gives the creditor more flexibility:

> *Following an Event of Default, Lender may in its sole discretion demand payment of all Borrower's Obligations then outstanding.*

Each type of acceleration clause has its pros and cons. An automatic acceleration clause benefits a secured party by relieving it of the burden of finding out that an event of default has occurred and notifying the debtor that it is now in default. But security agreements list so many things as events of default that an event frequently occurs without being sufficiently serious to make a secured party want to end the relationship—which likely also closes down debtor's business—by accelerating the loan and foreclosing on the collateral. Additionally, a lender's failure to exercise its remedies when it is entitled to provides an opening for the debtor to argue that the lender waived its rights.

An optional acceleration clause, in contrast, gives the lender flexibility in deciding whether to accelerate in the face of an event of default. However, that lender must also take some clear action that notifies debtor of the actual acceleration, unless state law allows a debtor to waive that notice. An optional acceleration clause that has a debtor waive notice regarding acceleration could read as follows:

> *Following an Event of Default, Lender may in its sole discretion demand payment of all Borrower's Obligations then outstanding, without presentment, demand, protest, or notice of any kind, all of which Borrower waives.*

Remember that when a lender invokes an acceleration clause improperly, then the only amount due is the amount that the debtor has not yet paid.

3. Repossession & Commercially Reasonable Disposition

Good transactional lawyers know the substantive law applicable to their transactions and then plan and structure transactions to take advantage of favorable law (e.g., tax effects, validity of liquidated damages provisions) and to avoid, or "draft around," unfavorable law. In secured transactions, security agreements often spell out the method by which the secured creditor can repossess and dispose of the collateral. Article 9 also specifies particular rights and duties that can be addressed in a security agreement and ones that are immutable.

a. Repossession

Secured parties—unlike most parties seeking to enforce a contract—do not have to notify their debtors that they are declaring default before they exercise their self-help rights to repossession. After repossession, however, a secured party must comply with §9–611 by notifying debtors of the time and method of disposition

Security agreement remedial provisions also generally specify whether the remedies listed are automatic or elective on the part of the creditor and whether the remedies are mutually exclusive or cumulative with one another and with the statutory rights and duties provided in Article 9. As you review and edit the template in the student assignment, be sure to consider the legality and enforceability of remedies as well. The most effective ones that counsel for the bank can imagine may be unenforceable or of limited enforceability.

A final note about default and remedies: The secured creditor should draft its notice of default—generally in the form of a letter— in unequivocal language and track the language and requirements of the contract exactly. There is no need to take an especially kind or insulting tone. A neutral description of the contract will suffice, which lists the pertinent provisions, the event of default that has occurred, a declaration of the default, an election of remedies, if needed, and any demand for action. Transmit the notice of default exactly as specified in the contract. Failure to strictly adhere to the contractual requirements affords the defaulting party a defense to enforcement and may allow additional time to cure and reinstate the agreement.

b. Commercially Reasonable Disposition

In our hypothetical, after debtor defaults, both the debtor and the bank have a strong interest in the bank getting as much money as possible for the collateral. The debtor hardware store does not want to be liable for a deficiency, and the personal guaranty in exercise #7 makes Bianca Bolt personally liable for part or all of the deficiency. Because unsecured claims are difficult to collect, FNB would also like to get a good price for the collateral. But Bianca Bolt's personal guaranty may moot that concern for the same reasons that it escalates her interest in selling the collateral for top dollar.

Throughout this book, we have assumed that Bianca Bolt has more clout in negotiations with FNB than debtors usually do with their lenders. In her quest to exercise that power, Bianca's research on how to get the best price for the collateral might pull up this article from the *Houston Chronicle*:

How Do I Sell a Small Retail Business?[43]
by Jessica Jones, studioD

Before putting your retail business up for sale, it is important to determine how much the store is worth. The length of time you have been in business, the demand for the types of goods and services you sell, the local commercial real estate market and annual profits are all factors you should consider when pricing your business. Overpricing may lead to few offers, while underpricing your retail business may cause you to lose money.

43   *How Do I Sell a Small Retail Business?* Jessica Jones, Leaf Group © 2010 Leaf Group, Ltd. U.S.A. All rights reserved. Reprinted with permission.

Step 1

Create a business profile for potential buyers that summarizes how your retail business operates. Include the types of goods and services provided and a description of your customer base. Include a copy of tax records, a list of annual business expenses and profits and loss statements for the past three years. Use this information to show buyers the potential profitability of your retail business and the amount of money needed to maintain the business properly.

Step 2

Create a list of business assets to include in the sale. Assets may include company vehicles; display items such as shelving, mannequins and clothing racks; cash registers; sales counters; cleaning supplies; and unsold inventory.

Step 3

Hire a business appraisal specialist to determine a fair price for your business. A business appraisal specialist will review your business profile and your list of business assets, and will research the value of similar businesses in the area to determine a sales price. Price your retail business fairly and competitively to entice as many potential buyers as possible.

Step 4

Advertise the sale of your business using online business websites such as bizbuysell.com or businessmart.com, or hire a business broker to attract potential buyers.

• Skill: Anticipate, Allocate & Minimize Risk

Step 5

Thoroughly clean your retail space. Rent carpet cleaning equipment, wash windows and dust display cases, clothing racks and other display items. Clean all rooms and organize storage areas so buyers can see the amount of space available.

Step 6

Create a sales agreement that outlines the final sale price, list of assets included in the price and financial responsibility of the buyer. Financial responsibility includes down payment amounts and a payment installment schedule. Hire an attorney to review the sales agreement to ensure all areas of the sale are covered.

Step 7

Set a closing date to sign all paperwork and to hand over the keys to your business and assets listed in the sales agreement.

Now that you know more about the business elements of defining default and specifying its consequences, you can try to match those business goals to words on the page in the following problem.

Problem 6: Endgame Provisions for Security Agreement

Identify the function of the following endgame provisions, then edit them for formatting, clarity & concision.

a. The Borrower shall be in default under this Agreement upon the occurrence of any one or more of the following (each an "Event of Default"): (a) there occurs any failure to pay any amounts when due and owing under the Obligations; or (b) any representation or warranty made in this Agreement or in connection with this Agreement shall prove to have been false or misleading when made in any material respect; or (c) the Borrower fails to timely and properly observe, keep or perform, any term, covenant, agreement or condition in this Agreement, which failure is not cured within any express cure period . . .

b. Following an Event of Default, the Lender may, in the exercise of its sole and absolute discretion from time to time, without notice (i) exercise its rights and remedies as a secured party under the UCC and other applicable Law; (ii) suspend, terminate or limit any further loans or other extensions of credit under this Agreement; and (iii) all Obligations then outstanding shall immediately become due and payable without any further action of any kind and without presentment, demand, protest or notice of any kind, all of which are hereby expressly waived by the Borrower . . .

c. Notice mailed to Borrower, at its address as it appears in this Agreement, ten (10) days before the date of public sale of the Collateral or ten (10) days before the date after which private sale of the Collateral will take place shall constitute reasonable notice to the Borrower and shall comply with the provisions of the UCC.

Now that you have a sense of business issues that drive endgame provisions, and the lawyer's special role in helping clients think about topics they would prefer to avoid, all that remains before you negotiate these provisions is to review the legal rules that provide the backdrop for contractual clauses.

Part III: Legal Rules

As always, remember to comply with Article 9 requirements. Recall that UCC Article § 9-601 treats default as a threshold requirement. Secured parties have no right to exercise their self-help remedies under Part 6 until the debtor is in default of the terms of the security agreement. In practical terms, this rule leads secured parties to draft security agreements with so many events of default that they can cite a handful of them—or more—to increase the chance that the lender is acting with authority.

Recall as well that Article 9 does not give secured parties attorney's fees unless the contract provides for them. If the definition of "obligation" in your security agreement includes attorney's fees and costs that the lender incurs to collect on the debt, then FNB can apply proceeds of collateral disposition to reasonable attorney's fees and costs.

The bulk of your negotiations concern repossession and, especially, foreclosure. UCC § 9–602 makes some debtors' rights and secured parties' duties immutable. UCC § 9–603 qualifies this rule by providing that a security agreement can establish "standards" for debtors' rights and secured parties' duties as long as those standards are not "manifestly unreasonable."

Issues that can be addressed in the security agreement include:

- § 9–609 allows the parties to agree for the debtor to assemble the collateral and make it available to the secured party to repossess, but § 9–603(b) forbids creditors from trying to set standards about whether a repossession breaches the peace;

- § 9–612 sets 10 days as a presumptively reasonable amount of notice to debtor before the secured party sells or otherwise disposes of the collateral; and

- § 9–603 allows parties to contractually commit to a method of disposition, as long as it is not manifestly unreasonable.

Note also that § 9–624 allows a debtor to waive certain rights only after default: notice of disposition; mandatory disposition under § 9–620; and redemption rights under § 9–623. In other words, a debtor cannot waive those rights in a security agreement.

Part IV: Student Assignment: Negotiate & Draft Events of Default & Remedies

This exercise has two components: negotiating then drafting the endgame provisions regarding default.

A. Tips for the Exercise

Now that you are familiar with the drafting, business, and doctrinal constraints on defining default and the consequences of default, it is time to negotiate those provisions.

Confer with other students who represent FNB or the debtor and consider what could go wrong in the business of Urban Hardware. Consider both catastrophes—fire, flood, closure for violation of licensing requirements—and ordinary events like the debtor missing a single payment on the promissory note because Bianca Bolt forgot to send it in. List these events, then check them against the events of default in the template. Have you missed any, or added ones that the precedent drafter did not consider?

Prepare to negotiate on events and consequences of default. Students playing the role of FNB should determine which events of default are most important, and which ones that your client could negotiate away. Students playing the role of the debtor should likewise determine what kind of notice and cure to negotiate. Are some defaults more likely to happen by mistake, or less likely to cause a big loss to FNB, and thus could be carved out as subject to debtor's cure rights?

After you and the student representing the other side finish your negotiations, draft clauses establishing the events that constitute default and the consequences of debtor's default. Remember that "Events of Default" is a defined term, which you will use in the clauses governing the consequences of default. The remedies clauses address acceleration and commercially reasonable disposition. Assume that the debtor has some bargaining power and build in some debtor-protecting clauses such as optional acceleration that entitles the debtor to notice of FNB's intent to accelerate and a grace period or opportunity to cure on some of the events of default.

B. Drafting Tips

- Read the security agreement's endgame provisions and label them in the margins (i.e., SP's Notice of Disposition, or D waiver of claims).

- Consider re-organizing the document.

  - Could §1 on interpretation appear elsewhere? One option is to add a definitions article right after the words of agreement and put the interpretation section after definitions. Another is to put it at the end of the document with other interpretive clauses regarding modification, merger, and waiver.

  - Can you make the agreement more readable, with more white space and less block text? (Hint: tabulation and subheadings will help.)

- Keep in mind the relationship between endgame clauses and earlier provisions in the agreement.

  - Secured parties draft events of default clauses intending to rely on several of them in case of default. Consider including:

- a provision that cross references other representations, warranties, and covenants elsewhere in the security agreement; and

- a catch-all provision allowing FNB to declare default when it reasonably deems itself insecure about the prospect of repayment.

- Establish the relationship between the commercially reasonable method of disposition you define and the background rules of §§ 9–610 to 9–612. FNB will want to make sure that it has discretionary authority to dispose of the collateral in any other commercially reasonable manner per the parameters of Article 9 as well as the method that you specify as commercially reasonable in the security agreement.

C. Checklist for Endgame Provisions

❏ Events of Default defined

❏ i.e., breach of covenant or representations, cross-default, transferring collateral without prior written permission, etc.

❏ Cure for some or all events of default?

❏ Consequences of Default specified

❏ Acceleration (automatic or optional)

❏ Repossession

❏ Attorney's fees

❏ Disposition of collateral

❏ Notice to D

❏ Method of disposition

❏ Method of notice (method, when effective, in boilerplate)

D. Template

As with the other exercises, the template below is on the book website in downloadable form. The clauses not at issue in this assignment are deleted and noted only by headings. Cut and paste your redrafts from the earlier assignments before starting to edit the endgame provisions. Use the material in earlier chapters on formatting and document organization. As always write precisely, clearly, and consistently, edit out legalese, use the active voice, and express yourself as succinctly as possible.

LOAN AND SECURITY AGREEMENT

THIS LOAN AND SECURITY AGREEMENT (this "Agreement") is made this 12th day of June, 2017, by and between SECOND BANK OF SPRINGFIELD (the "Lender"), with a mailing address for the purposes of this Agreement at 123 Fake St., Springfield, NY 13333, Attn: Milhause Van Houten, and GLOBAL PAINT & HARDWARE, Inc. (d/b/a Global Club Hardware), a New York corporation (the "Borrower"), with a chief executive office and mailing address for the purposes of this Agreement of 747 Hammer Dr., Shelbyville, NY 13332.

RECITALS

A. The Borrower is engaged in the business of operating a Club Hardware store (the "Business") at the following location: 747 Hammer Dr., Shelbyville, NY 13332 (the "Business Premises").

B. The Borrower has applied to the Lender for a Loan in the original principal amount of $350,000 (the "Loan," and all other extensions of credit by the Lender to the Borrower being sometimes hereinafter referred to collectively as the "Loans").

C. The Lender is willing to provide the Loans on the condition that the Borrower enters into this Agreement, which shall, among other things, govern and secure the Loans.

NOW, THEREFORE, in consideration of the foregoing and of the mutual promises, covenants and agreements of the parties contained in this Agreement, the parties do agree as follows:

1. Interpretation. The Recitals accurately state the facts, circumstances and intentions of the parties and are hereby incorporated in this Agreement by this reference and made a part hereof. The headings in this Agreement are included in this Agreement for convenience only, shall not constitute a part of this Agreement for any other purpose, and shall not be deemed to affect the meaning or construction of any of the provisions hereof. All terms used in this Agreement which are defined by the New York Uniform Commercial Code ("UCC") shall have the same meanings as assigned to them by the UCC unless and to the extent varied by this Agreement.

2. [The Loans.]

3. [Creation of Security Interest.]

4. [Borrower Representations and Warranties regarding authority, etc.]

5. [Borrower Covenants regarding Reporting, etc.]

6. Default. The Borrower shall be in default under this Agreement and under each of the other Loan Documents upon the occurrence of any one or more of the following (each an "Event of Default"; any one or more collectively, "Events of Default"): (a) there occurs any failure to pay any amounts when due and owing under the Loans or the other Obligations; or (b) any representation or warranty made in this Agreement or in connection with this Agreement (including, without limitation, any opinion of counsel for the Borrower or other obligor to the Lender), any of the other Loan Documents, or the Obligations, shall prove to have been false or misleading when made (or, if applicable, when reaffirmed) in any material respect; or (c) the Borrower or any other obligor under the Loan Documents fails to timely and properly observe, keep or perform, any term, covenant, agreement or condition in this Agreement, in any of the other Loan Documents, which failure is not cured within any express cure period, or challenges the validity of any material provision of the Loan Documents; or (d) the Borrower transfers to or allows any of the Collateral to be located at a location other than a location expressly described in Section 5 of this Agreement; or (e) the Borrower or any other obligor under the Loan Documents suspends or terminates its business operations or liquidates, dissolves or terminates its existence or, if an individual, dies; or (f) the Borrower or any other obligor under the Loan Documents is in default under any indebtedness for borrowed money (other than the Loans); or (g) the Borrower or any other obligor under the Loan Documents is in default under any indebtedness, liabilities and obligations (other than the Loans) to the Lender; or (h) (1) the Borrower or any other obligor under the Loan Documents admits in writing its inability generally to pay its debts as they mature or shall make any assignment for the benefit of any of its creditors or (2) the Borrower or any other obligor under the Loan Documents is the subject of federal or state bankruptcy, insolvency, receivership or trustee proceedings (any Event of Default under this clause being sometimes referred to as an "Insolvency Default"); or (i) any of the Loan Documents shall for any reason (except to the extent permitted by its express terms) cease to be effec-

tive; or (j) unless the Lender has previously agreed otherwise in writing, the Lender at any time shall cease to have a valid and perfected first priority Lien on, or security interest in, any of the Collateral; or (k) the Borrower suffers, in the good faith judgment of the Lender, a material adverse change in the Borrower's financial condition or in the Lender's rights and remedies with respect to, or the value of, the Collateral.

7. Remedies.

7.1 Following an Event of Default, the Lender may, in the exercise of its sole and absolute discretion from time to time, without notice (i) exercise its rights and remedies as a secured party under the UCC and other applicable Laws and as otherwise set forth in the Loan Documents, (ii) suspend, terminate or limit any further loans or other extensions of credit under this Agreement and under any of the other Loan Documents, provided further that upon the occurrence of an Event of Default specified in subsections 6 (g) and (h) of Section 6 (Default) of this Agreement, any commitment or agreement to provide additional credit contained in this Agreement or the other Loan Documents shall automatically terminate and all Obligations then outstanding shall immediately become due and payable without any further action of any kind and without presentment, demand, protest or notice of any kind, all of which are hereby expressly waived by the Borrower, and/or (iii) declare all the rest or any portion of the Note and all other Obligations remaining unpaid, whether due or not, immediately due and payable without notice or demand to the Borrower.

7.2 In the case of an Event of Default, the Lender may enter upon the Borrower's premises at any time, using such force as the Lender deems necessary (but in no event causing a breach of the peace), and seize the Collateral, removing it at Borrower's cost and expense, all without notice or judicial process. If an Event of Default has occurred, the Lender may require Borrower at Borrower's expense to assemble the Collateral, as well as all of its books and records pertaining to accounts and notes receivable, and make it available to the Lender at a place designated by the Lender, and it shall not be necessary for the Lender to remove the Collateral from Borrower's premises but the Borrower shall permit the Lender and hereby authorize and empower the Lender, without the need or necessity for any notice or court proceeding or the requirement that the Lender resort to judicial process of any kind, to keep the Collateral in the place of business of the Borrower as above in this Agreement identified and to remove any locks thereon and put its own lock on such premises or on any other premises where such Collateral may be located, thereby denying access to Borrower, until five (5) days after the sale of the Collateral. The Borrower waives any and all claims and causes of action of any nature, kind, or description which it may have or may claim to have against the Lender or its representatives, by reason of taking possession of (with or without judicial process) or selling, maintaining and storing the Collateral on Borrower's property or otherwise, or any claims arising from damage done to Borrower's premises or other property in seizing the Collateral.

7.3 The Lender may remedy in any manner or waive any Event of Default of Borrower without waiving the default remedied or any other prior or subsequent default.

7.4 Notice mailed to Borrower, at its address as it appears in this Agreement, ten (10) days before the date of public sale of the Collateral or ten (10) days before the date after which private sale of the Collateral will take place shall constitute reasonable notice to the Borrower and shall comply with the provisions of the UCC, except with respect to any Collateral constituting perishable goods, for which the Lender shall not be required to provide such prior notice. In addition to the foregoing, the Lender shall be entitled to give such notice in any other commercially reasonable manner as the Lender may elect from time to time.

7.5 If for any reason the Collateral set forth shall fail, upon disposal by the Lender for default, to satisfy the Note, the obligation, and all other debts, loans, notes or other monies, payment of which is secured by this Agreement or allowable under the UCC, then the Borrower shall pay the Lender the deficiency upon demand. However, if after disposal of the Collateral and after payment of all sums secured by this Agreement and otherwise payable under the UCC there is a surplus of funds, then the Lender agrees to pay the same over to the Borrower, or to whomever may be legally entitled to the same.

7.6 The Borrower does hereby covenant that if there shall occur any Event of Default under the terms of any of the Loan Documents, or in the event any money or property of the Borrower in the possession of the Lender is garnished or attached (which the Borrower agrees is a default under this Agreement), any indebtedness owed by the Lender to the Borrower or any property of the Borrower in the hands of the Lender may be applied to the payment in whole or in part of the Obligations in such order as the Lender may elect in the exercise of its sole and absolute discretion from time to time.

7.7 Each and every right granted to the Lender under any Loan Document, or allowed it by law or equity shall be cumulative of each other and may be exercised in addition to any and all other rights of the Lender. No delay in exercising any right, power or privilege shall operate as a waiver thereof, nor shall any single or partial exercise by the Lender of any right preclude any other or future exercise thereof or the exercise of any other right nor shall any single or partial exercise of any right, power or privilege hereunder preclude any other or further exercise thereof or the exercise of any other right, power or privilege and no waiver shall be established hereunder by repetition in the course of dealing. The Borrower expressly waives any presentment, demand, protest or other notice of any kind, including but not limited to notice of intent to accelerate and notice of acceleration. No notice to or demand on the Borrower in any case shall, of itself, entitle the Borrower to any other or future notice or demand in similar or other circumstances expressly required in this Agreement. Without limiting the generality of the foregoing, the Lender may proceed against the Borrower with or without proceeding against any guarantor, surety, indemnitor or any other person who may be liable for all or any part of the Obligations.

8.   [Other Agreements.]

8.1 [Notice.]

8.2 [Attorneys' Fees] [Lender as Borrower's Attorney-in-Fact.]

8.3 [Release.] [Modification and Waiver]

8.4 [Survival of Obligations.]

8.5 [Successors & Assigns.]

8.6 [Choice of Law.]

8.7 [Severability.]

8.8 [Modification.]

8.9 [Jury Waiver.]

IN WITNESS WHEREOF, the parties hereto have caused this Agreement to be executed under seal and delivered as of the day and year first above written.

GLOBAL PAINT & HARDWARE, Inc.
d/b/a Global Club Hardware

By: _____
      Patricia Bouvier
      President

SECOND BANK OF SPRINGFIELD

By: _____
      Milhause Van Houten
      Senior Vice President

Personal Guaranty & Boilerplate
*Skill: Distinguish Individual from Entity Liability
& Finetune Standard Terms*

Overview

THIS EXERCISE involves a personal guaranty, which is common in transactions like Bolt Urban Hardware's credit arrangement with FNB. As a business matter a personal guaranty requires Bianca Bolt to repay the bank if the debtor fails to meet its obligations. In the language of transactional lawyers, the guaranty creates a secondary obligation—usually a payment obligation—to support the primary obligation between the lender and the debtor. Through the guaranty Bianca Bolt can assume various levels of risk, from an unconditional promise to cover the Store's obligations to a more limited willingness to pay only if the debtor cannot, and perhaps also capping Bianca's exposure at a fixed amount rather than the total.

This chapter also covers so-called boilerplate provisions that appear toward the end of most agreements. These clauses—often dismissed as mere "housekeeping provisions"—play an important role so are better described as endgame and interpretive provisions. While they cover a wide range of topics including assignment and severability, this exercise focuses on five types of clause that indicate how to perform, the relevance of the parties' behavior and communications outside the writing, and how to resolve disputes.

As with the other exercises, Part I covers contract drafting issues, first the concepts of secondary obligation and interpretive provisions, and then the essential drafting skills of limiting a guaranty with techniques like carve-outs, baskets, and caps, and ways to fine-tune interpretive clauses. Part II recaps the legal rules governing guaranties in secured transactions. Finally, Part III pulls it all together by having you negotiate the terms of the guaranty and interpretive provisions and edit a template to reflect your agreement.

Part I: Guaranties & Interpretive Provisions Explained

Both personal guaranties and interpretive provisions at the end of a contract arise out of endgame concerns. If the debtor defaults and cannot pay its obligations, a personal guaranty shifts that responsibility to an individual—here Bianca Bolt. Along the same lines, so-called boilerplate provisions regarding issues like notice, merger, and modification or waiver tend to come up only when the parties disagree about the terms of their arrangement, often when their dispute is so irresolvable that the parties litigate. Accordingly, the drafting material in this exercise focuses first on guaranties and then on how interpretive provisions can prevent disputes from arising or escalating.

A. Guaranties

The first step of drafting a personal guaranty is to understand how it operates. This section describes common types of guaranties and the difference between guaranties and indemnification.

In addition to providing a Plan B to collect a debt, personal guaranties provide a powerful incentive for a flesh-and-blood person like Bianca Bolt who runs a business to run it well, if only to make sure that the bank does not come against her home, car, and other personal assets for repayment. Bianca's personal responsibility to pay at least part of the debt shapes both day to day business operations and serious violations of the security agreement by, say, transferring collateral without FNB's permission.

The business issues here are twofold: (1) whether the bank or Bianca Bolt personally bears the risk of the Store not repaying the loan; and (2) the extent of that risk. As explained at the end of this section, the contractual concept of indemnification is related but distinct.

Types of Guaranty

Guaranties take various forms. They range from the absolute guaranty that provides the beneficiary with the most protection possible to conditional and restricted guaranties that impose limits on a guarantor's liability through conditions or monetary caps. Though transactional attorneys often speak in colorful language about "springing," "shrinking," "creeping," or "burn down" guaranties, this list briefly describes this range in more prosaic and descriptive terms. While guaranties can secure any kind of obligation, we focus here on lender/borrower guaranties:

- *Absolute Guaranty.* An absolute guaranty has the guarantor promise to pay or perform the original debtor's obligations when that debtor defaults on its obligation to the lender. Drafters commonly use the phrase "absolute and unconditional" to maximize the chance that the court will treat the guaranty as absolute.

- *Conditional Guaranty.* A conditional guaranty requires some contingent event to happen—other that the primary debtor's default—or the lender to perform some act before the guarantor will be liable. For example, a "springing" guaranty could require payment if the original debtor files for bankruptcy, "shrinking" guaranties diminish liability as the principal shrinks, and "creeping" guaranties increase liability.

- *Payment Guaranty.* A payment guaranty obliges the guarantor to pay the debt at maturity, which may happen post-default if the lender accelerates the original debtor's obligation. As soon as default on that primary obligation occurs, the guarantor's obligation is fixed and the lender does not have to make demand on the primary obligor.

- *Collection Guaranty.* A collection guaranty is a guarantor's promise to pay if the lender cannot collect the claim from the original debtor, and requires the lender to try to collect from the original debtor, usually after a suit and exhaustion of remedies.

- *Continuing Guaranty.* A continuing guaranty extends beyond a particular transaction to cover future dealings such as a series of transactions. It could extend for an indefinite period and include new debts incurred by the debtor even without new consideration.

- *Restricted Guaranty.* Restrictions on a guaranty can limit the number of transactions, the amount of money guarantied, or the duration of the guaranty. For example, a "burn down" guaranty restricts the amount guaranteed to an amount determined by how much principal the original debtor had paid on the loan.

In addition, the guarantor's promise to pay a debtor's obligation can be secured with collateral. In that situation the document is both a personal guaranty and a security agreement. It must comply with UCC Article 9 requirements for the security interest to attach to the guarantor's personal property and with real estate law if the collateral is real property such as the guarantor's house.

Look over the list above and consider which kind of guaranty FNB would seek, and which kind Bianca Bolt would prefer. Consider arguments that you could make or anticipate the other side will make in negotiations. You will need to use mechanisms that transactional attorneys call carve-outs, baskets, and caps to draft a guaranty that restricts the amount of money that Bianca must pay, or limits the time of that liability.

B. Drafting Technique: Carve-Outs, Baskets, & Caps

Drafters use carve-outs, baskets, and caps to qualify an obligation, whether of guarantor or any other kind of contracting party. A carve out removes—or carves out—part of a right or restriction. For example:

> *Borrower shall not sell any of its assets, except for any equipment that has reached its end-of-life status or a status of technical obsolescence.*

A basket, in contrast, gives a party a right to deviate from a covenant's restriction by a specified amount. For example:

> *Borrower shall not sell any of its assets, except for equipment in an aggregate amount not exceeding $15,000.*

If it occurs to you that you could add on a provision carving out situations where the lender provides prior written permission for the disposition, then you are getting the hang of carve-outs and baskets.

Caps provide a third way to limit an obligation. A cap limits the amount of liability a party bears. In a guaranty, a guarantor like Bianca Bolt could cap her obligation to cover for the original debtor's debt at a set amount. She could set it lower than the amount of the promissory note, on the ground that the lender should be able to satisfy much of the original debtor's obligation by disposing of the collateral. Moreover, just as lenders want a guaranty in part to nudge the original debtor toward good behavior—lest the people who run the business be personally liable—debtors seek to create incentives for lenders to get as good a price as they can for the collateral instead of disposing it with little effort and the plan to recover through the guaranty.

A cap on a guarantor's liability could read

> *The Guarantor's liability under this Limited Guaranty will not exceed the sum of $200,000 plus any costs or expenses, including reasonable attorneys' fees and costs, incurred by or on behalf of the Guaranteed Party to the Guarantor's obligations under this Limited Guaranty (the **"Cap"**).*

Carve-outs, baskets, and caps provide language you should use in negotiating the limits on Bianca Bolt's personal liability to FNB.

Problem 7: Carve-outs, Baskets & Caps

You represent Bonnie, the president of Bonnie's Beautiful Blooms ("BBB"). You and the bank lending to BBB have negotiated a personal guaranty in which Bonnie will pay BBB's obligation to the bank in the following circumstances. Draft the clauses that reflect these terms, writing one as a carve-out, one as a basket, and the third as a cap. Refer to the parties as Guarantor, BBB, and Bank.

    a. The Bank can collect money from the Guarantor, but the amount is reduced by the amount that the Bank did get or could have gotten from conducting a commercially reasonable disposition of the Collateral.

b. The Guarantor promises to notify the Bank of all material claims that arise against her after signing the Guaranty, "material" meaning any claim in excess of $10,000.

c. The Guarantor's liability to the bank, including reasonable attorney's fees and costs, will not exceed $500,000.

The substantive provisions that qualify Bianca's personal liability will be your main focus as you negotiate and draft the guaranty in Part III. But you should also review and edit the interpretive provisions at the end of the agreement to ensure that they reflect your client's interests. The following section explains what you will be looking for and wanting to change, depending on whether you represent FNB or Bianca Bolt.

C. Interpretive Provisions[1]

Never take boilerplate for granted or simply incorporate standard provisions without thought and analysis. Transactional attorneys too often treat them that way by giving them a heading like "Miscellaneous." They are not. They contain crucial provisions that can determine whether the parties' conduct as well as the writing can provide terms for their agreement.

An opposing party may even try to slip in a one-sided provision, such as one that requires only it, and not your side, to agree to modify in writing. Along the same lines, one bank's security agreement required its borrower to give written notice but allowed the bank to provide oral notice:

> *Any notice by the Bank to the Borrower may be oral and is deemed to have been duly given to and received by the Borrower at the time of the oral communication.*

Read these interpretive clauses carefully to make sure that they reflect the parties' intent.

Common provisions are described below, starting with notice because it is the most substantive of the provisions and most likely to guide the parties' performance. Make sure that the people involved know and understand the proper method of giving notice.

1. Notice

Notice provisions typically include four elements that reflect the who, where, what, when, and how of notice: (1) describe to the name and ad-

---

1   Based on Haggard & Kuney, *Legal Drafting* pp. 39–41.

dress to whom the notice must be sent; (2) require a writing; (3) say when notice is effective; and (4) specify the means by which the notice is sent.

Although people conduct much of their business on email or other electronic means of communication, some drafters still require hard copy notice to prevent notices getting caught in spam filters or overlooked among accumulated email. For example:

> *All notices and other communications (**"Notices"**) required or permitted under this Agreement must be in writing and will be effective upon receipt at a party's address as set forth in the preamble or to another address that a party designates in writing. Notices may be hand-delivered, sent by facsimile transmission with confirmation of delivery and a copy sent by first-class mail, or sent by nationally recognized overnight courier service.*

In a large transaction, a notice provision often requires notice be sent to a party and a copy sent to that party's attorneys to reduce the chance that a notice gets overlooked.

A notice provision that allows for email could provide:

> *Any notice pursuant to this Agreement must be in writing or by machine-readable electronic transmission (**"Electronic Notice"**), and is deemed to have been given and received by a party when it has been sent to the address named above in the preamble or another address that the recipient designates by first class mail, or if given by hand or by Electronic Notice, when actually received by that party and its counsel at the offices specified in Section III(B), below.*

• SKILL: DISTINGUISH INDIVIDUAL FROM ENTITY LIABILITY & FINETUNE STANDARD TERMS

The parties may well review these notice provisions in the ordinary course of performing the contract. The remaining interpretive terms, in contrast, are likely irrelevant unless the parties face a serious disagreement. Contrary to popular belief, these clauses could make an enormous difference in how that dispute gets resolved.

2. Significance of Written Terms

Contract law generally treats written terms as the best reflection of the parties' intent and requires some types of agreement like land transactions and sales of goods for $500 or more to be memorialized in signed writings to be enforceable. However the parties' behavior and the commercial context can also determine terms. Oral agreements—side deals—that parties make as they negotiate and execute documents may clarify what the written terms mean, as can procedures they have followed in prior transactions. During the performance parties may modify their agreement, either in words—oral or written—or implicitly through conduct known as the course of performance.

Contract doctrine has different terms for different types of evidence from outside a written agreement, and transactional lawyers use particular clauses to address each kind of communication. Agreements made prior to or contemporaneously with signing the agreement—oral or written—are known as parol evidence. A merger clause—also known as an integration clause—limits the legal relevance of parol evidence. Modification is an agreement after the contract is formed to change the terms, and a no-oral-modification or NOM clause requires those modifications to be in writing, usually signed by both parties. Waiver is the intentional relinquishment of a known right such as a bank not declaring default after a single missed payment, and loan agreements typically include anti-waiver clauses.

a. Merger Clause

Merger clauses state that the parties' entire agreement is merged into this one writing. They apply only to agreements made before or at the time that the parties sign the contract. Common law and the UCC provide slightly different rules that govern when a written agreement provides all contractual terms, excluding anything from outside the agreement. For example, UCC Article 2 provides terms of art that a drafter can use in a merger clause. If the parties want to include consistent additional terms, then the merger clause could say that the writing represents the "final" statement of the parties' agreement. Drafters who seek to exclude consistent additional terms use the phrase "complete and exclusive" to express that intent.

In practice, however, drafters tend to use terms like "entire" and "supersedes" to prevent a party from even alleging that the agreement also includes terms from outside the written agreement.

For example, a loan and security agreement provided:

> *This Agreement and the Note contain the entire agreement between the parties and supersede all prior or contemporaneous oral or written negotiations, agreements, representations, and understandings regarding this Agreement and the Note.*

When reviewing a contract make sure that the merger clause reflects your client's intent. Remember that your client may be the one that wants to rely on agreements outside of the writing. Merger clauses do not foreclose the possibility of litigation about extrinsic evidence, but they provide strong evidence of what the parties intended to be part of their agreement, and what they intentionally excluded.

b. No-Oral-Modification

Modification looks at communication or behavior that happens after the contract is formed. Most written contracts require that any modifications be in writing, a clause that transactional attorneys call a NOM clause, for "no oral modification." Although UCC §2–209(2) recognizes the efficacy of these no-oral-modification provisions, the courts in both sales and non-sales contract contexts can be liberal in finding a waiver of the NOM clause. Nevertheless, NOM clauses function as a useful prophylactic.

An NOM clause could read:

> *No modification of this Agreement is effective unless made in a writing signed by both parties.*

Security agreements, usually drafted by lenders with lender-friendly terms, sometimes provide that only the secured party is required to sign modifications, allowing the lender to offer oral evidence or an unsigned writing to prove a debtor's agreement to modify the terms. A one-sided NOM clause could provide:

> *No modification of this Agreement is effective unless made in a writing signed by the Secured Party.*

Note that these provisions address only modification. Because modification and waiver are closely related issues—and the same set of facts can justify either argument—drafters often include anti-waiver provisions in the NOM clause. For purposes of understanding the difference between modification and waiver, waiver clauses are discussed separately below.

c. No Waiver

The main difference between waiver and modification is how long it lasts. Say that a loan requires that the debtor make payments on the first of the month. If the lender accepts two payments that the debtor made five days late, the lender will argue that it is a waiver of the timing provision regarding payment, and the debtor will see it as a modification. If the court treats it as a waiver, then the lender could argue that it merely waived the payment term for those two late payments but can insist on prompt delivery for subsequent payments. If instead a court finds that the parties modified the payment date term, then the debtor could have a five day grace period for the remaining life of the contract.

While lenders generally prefer to construe leniency as a waiver rather than a modification, security agreements—like many contracts—typically include anti-waiver clauses. A debtor's performance is repeated many times, from making payments to other obligations like quarterly reporting on inventory levels or account balances. Accordingly, the contract often provides that a lender's failure to insist on strict performance in one instance is not a waiver of its right to insist on strict performance if another default occurs.

A general anti-waiver provision could provide:

> *No waiver of any provision of this Agreement is effective unless executed in writing by the party against whom the change is asserted. Any waiver is effective only in the specific instance that it is given.*

Add-on language to protect secured parties could specify common circumstances that do not constitute waivers:

No notice to the debtor entitles the debtor to any other notice. Any forbearance, failure or delay by the Bank in exercising any right is not deemed a waiver, and any single or partial exercise by the Bank of any right does not waive full exercise of that right until specifically waived by the Bank in writing.

Despite these detailed clauses, waiver clauses are not fool-proof. Parties can waive an anti-waiver clause just as they can waive other provisions. The drafter's duty here is to decrease the chance of disputes, because complete avoidance is not possible.

3. Third Parties—Assignment and Delegation

The parties may want to expressly permit or prohibit the assignment of contract rights or the delegation of contract duties to a third party. Dealing with the issue in this manner is much easier than litigating it under the murky common law rules on assignment and delegation. Although courts frequently construe a reference to an assignment of the contract to refer to both rights and duties, the drafter should deal separately with the assignment of rights and the delegation of duties.

Here is sample anti-assignment language:

The Bank may assign to any person any Indebtedness of the Debtor, and the assignee will succeed to all the powers and rights of the Bank. The debtor may not assign or transfer any of its rights or obligations without the prior written consent of the Bank.

4. Survivability and Severability

Survivability and severability sound alike but cover different issues. Under a survivability clause, the agreement remains in effect despite the incapacity or death of one or more of the parties of the contact. Severability, in contrast, looks to the continued validity of a contract when one of its clauses is struck down as unenforceable.

The survivability clause could be headed "Successors and Assigns" and read:

> *The words "Debtor" and "Guarantor" in this Agreement include their heirs, executors, administrators, legal representatives, and all persons claiming by and through them.*

A severability clause, in contrast, typically provides:

> *The provisions of this Agreement are intended by the parties to be severable and the unenforceability of any provision does not invalidate the remainder of this Agreement.*

The parties could also prohibit severance and partial enforcement. Whether the clause allows or prohibits severance, in most cases it simply mirrors the contract law default rule that would be applied even in the absence of a clause. That is, if a court has declared one provision unenforceable, the court will usually treat the other provisions of the contract as still in force unless doing so would destroy the purpose of the contract or create unfairness. If, however, there is any question about how the default severability rule would apply if a particular term in the contract is declared void, then the drafter should make severability express.

• SKILL: DISTINGUISH INDIVIDUAL FROM ENTITY LIABILITY & FINETUNE STANDARD TERMS

5. Dispute Resolution: Choice of Law & Forum Selection

Choice of law and forum selection clauses save the parties from arguments about what substantive law governs disputes arising out of the agreement and also determines the forum for dispute resolution. Absent choice of law and forum selection clauses the parties could spend considerable time and money litigating these issues under common law choice of law principles.

The drafter should carefully compare the law in the various jurisdictions that might qualify. Although the courts generally defer to the desires of the parties on this matter, choice-of-law and forum selection provisions must bear some relationship to the transaction. Since a court might refuse to defer to the parties' choice of law, the drafter should draft with the default choice in mind.

For example:

> *All disputes between the parties concerning this Agreement or any other matter arising out of this Agreement are governed by the internal laws of the State of New York, without regard to principles of conflicts of law.*

While "concerning" and "arising out of" seem like duplicative legalese, both phrases are necessary to ensure that both contract and tort claims such as fraud in the inducement are covered by the clause.

Now that you know the basic types of guaranties and interpretive provisions is it time to review the relevant legal rules that will shape your negotiation and drafting.

Part II: LEGAL RULES

Personal guaranties raise classic common law issues like the statue of frauds and proof of consideration as well as compliance with Article 9.

A. Signed writing

A personal guaranty is essentially a suretyship in which the guarantor ensures performance by the original debtor. Suretyship falls within the statute of frauds, so guaranties must be evidenced by a writing signed by the guarantor that indicates that a contract has been formed.[2]

While a notary generally is not required to make a personal guaranty legally binding, a good number of lenders include that provision, and add in a signature block a witness, or both. Why might a lender want to add in notarization or another witness provision?

B. Recitation of Consideration

Because a guaranty is a secondary obligation, it is often unclear what the guarantor gets out of the transaction, and thus whether the agreement lacks consideration and is therefore unenforceable. Generally speaking, a guaranty given at the same time as the underlying obligation does not need a separate consideration.[3] While jurisdictions vary as to the significance of recitations of consideration in a guaranty, lenders often insert them to ward off claims of lack of consideration.

---

2   *Restatement (3d) of Suretyship* §11 (1996); NY Gen'l Oblig §5-701 (2016).

3   *Restatement (3d) of Suretyship* §7 (1996).

C. Distinguishing Absolute from Restricted Guaranties

The most important substantive issue is whether Bianca Bolt's personal guaranty is absolute or restricted. Beware using both terms, lest the ambiguity lead to litigation.

In one case a personal guaranty included both clauses describing it as "unconditional" and also included a "burndown" personal guaranty that reduced the guarantor's liability in proportion to the debtor's payment of the loan's principal. After protracted litigation the court concluded that the guaranty was absolute—a payment guaranty instead of a collection guaranty—but clear drafting could have kept the parties out of court.[4]

If you negotiate a restricted guaranty, you should specify the nature of that restriction. For example, identify what FNB must do if you require FNB to first try to collect from Bolt's Urban Hardware, LLC before demanding that Bianca Bolt pay the obligation. A phrase such as "prompt exercise of best efforts" to collect from the primary debtor imposes a general obligation on FNB. That clause also could require FNB to comply with the commercially reasonable methods of disposition specified in the security agreement before it seeks to collect from Bianca Bolt personally under the guaranty.

D. Article 9 Relevance

Article 9 trumps suretyship rules to the extent that the two are inconsistent.[5] But Article 9's rules that protect secondary obligors give the parties a good measure of contractual freedom to determine the extent of a personal guaranty.

---

4   *Bank of America National Trust & Savings v. Schulson*, 305 Ill. App.3d 941 (1999), modified and reh'g denied (June 30, 1999), reh'g denied (Sept. 9, 1999), appeal denied, 186 Ill.2d 565 (1999).

5   *Restatement (3d) of Suretyship §3* (1996).

In exercise #6 you negotiated and drafted endgame provisions with only the lender and debtor in mind as you considered provisions such as FNB's obligation to give the Store some period of notice—perhaps 10 or 20 days—before disposing of the collateral post-default. Now you have a third party to this transaction, Bianca Bolt in her personal capacity. As guarantor of the Store's debt, she will want to enjoy the rights that the Store negotiated for itself in the security agreement endgame provisions.

Article 9 provides some default rules that benefit individual guarantors even if the security agreement ignores them. Recall that §9–102 refers to guarantors as "secondary obligors," and that under Part 6 secondary obligors enjoy many of the rights that protect debtors. For example, §9–611 requires secured parties to notify secondary obligors of the time and method of collateral disposition post-default, and §9–625 gives secondary obligors the same rights as debtors to contest commercially unreasonable dispositions.

Accordingly, it is in both FNB and Bianca Bolt's interest to negotiate notice to her personally as well as to the Store in the event of default. You should incorporate the personal guaranty by reference into the security agreement, and also edit the security agreement's notice provisions to include Bianca Bolt personally as well as any other guarantor who comes into the transaction. As you edit all of the documents in prior exercises to compile the portfolio in exercise #10, make sure that the boilerplate or interpretive provisions in them are consistent with each other.

E. Difference between Guaranty & Indemnification

Though indemnification and guaranties are related concepts—both of them require a person to cover a loss incurred by someone else—they differ in important ways. Indemnification is a primary obligation, which does not depend on the borrower's obligation. Indemnification provisions commonly appear in publication agreements. For example, an author generally indemnifies the publisher against losses resulting from the claims made by third parties:

> *Author shall indemnify Publisher against all damages suffered and expenses incurred by Publisher, including reasonable attorney fees, resulting from Author's breach of these representations and warranties.*

If that primary obligation to publish the book is not enforceable for any reason, the indemnification could remain valid.

A guaranty, in contrast, involves three parties. Under the terms of the note and security agreement, FNB is the lender and the Bolt's Urban Hardware, LLC is the debtor. Bianca Bolt signs both documents as an agent of the Store, not in her individual capacity. The bank, Store and Bianca get different labels in the guaranty. In a guaranty, FNB is the beneficiary, Bianca is the guarantor, and the Store is the primary obligor. As guarantor, Bianca promises to pay or otherwise perform if the Store does not. Because the Store's liability is primary, Bianca's obligations may be reduced or extinguished if the primary obligation is void.

Part III: Student Assignment

A. Negotiate the Guaranty Terms

You are now ready to negotiate the guaranty. The main business issues are: (1) whether the guaranty is absolute or restrictive; and (2) if it is restricted the nature of the limitation, such as a monetary limit or a requirement that FNB first exhaust its remedies against the Store. (Your professor may require one restriction, leaving you to determine its details.)

If you represent Bianca Bolt, make two lists, one that specifies protections that Bianca must have and the other of less important issues that she is willing to negotiate away. If you represent FNB, do the same on its behalf. Both sides should review the general provisions at the end of the template to see if they reflect the parties' intent regarding notice, extrinsic evidence, and other issues.

If your professor gives you instructions from your client, comply with the rules of professional responsibility and do not disclose confidential communications except to the extent necessary to complete the negotiation.

B. Draft the Guaranty

It is time to put that agreement into writing. Edit the template below, which is available in downloadable form on the book website. As you review the template, note the difference between it and the other agreements you have worked with.

Be sure to use precise language in defining the extent of Bianca Bolt's guaranty. If it is restricted by monetary amount, duration, or the requirement that FNB tries to collect against the Store before demanding payment from Bianca personally, use adjectives like "restricted" or "conditional" and delete all references to the guaranty being "absolute."

Applicable contract concepts are covenants, declarations, conditions, carve-outs, baskets, and caps. Bianca covenants to pay the obligation if the Store does not. Interpretive provisions address issues like merger. Conditions determine triggering events for Bianca's liability. Finally, carve-outs, baskets and caps provide the drafting techniques to limit Bianca Bolt's liability.

Cut and paste the names of the parties from the security agreement and add Bianca Bolt as a new party to the transaction. Recitals could describe the relation of the personal guaranty to the rest of the transaction.

C. Tips for the Exercise

- Consider improving the format by adding tabulation, putting the headings in bold font and adding headings where they will aid the reader.

- Conform the format across the documents in this transaction so that paragraph numbering is in the same format.

- Notice that the statement of consideration is at the end of the guaranty, in the final article titled "General Provisions." Consider moving it to Article 1 or 2, consistent with the general rule that consideration is specified at the outset of most agreements. Consider also why this template places issues like anti-waiver protections for the lender in the substance of the contract. As discussed in exercise #5, a common way to organize a document is to place more important provisions before less important ones and substance before procedure. Consider how to reorganize the sections so that, for example, choice of law is toward the end of the agreement. Be sure to edit the headings to reflect your revisions.

- Be sure to make the signature block conforms to conventions for Bianca Bolt to be bound by the agreement in her individual capacity. Exercise #1 provides an example.

- The notary's authentication and a witness for the personal guaranty is generally not required by law, but lenders often insert it to preclude a guarantor from claiming that her signature was forged. Decide whether you want to include these provisions. If so, make up a notary seal and execute it as if a notary authenticated the guaranty, and also make up the name of a disinterested person who can serve as a witness.

D. Checklist

Guaranty

❏ Absolute or Restricted?

❏ Specify at least one restrictions if required by your instructor (amount, time for collection, etc.)

❏ Delete references to other form of guaranty

Boilerplate

❏ Adapt template

❏ Conform boilerplate to note and security agreement provisions

❏ Merger clause reflects parties' intent

❏ Notice clause identifies who, what, and where to send, and when effective

❏ Anti-waiver clause

❏ Choice of Law clauses exempt local rules regarding choice of law

UNCONDITIONAL GUARANTY

Guarantor	Patricia Bouvier
Borrower	Global Paint & Hardware, Inc. d/b/a Global Club Hardware
Lender	Second Bank of Springfield
Date	June 12, 2017
Note Amount	$350,000.00

1. GUARANTY:

Guarantor unconditionally guaranties payment to Lender of all amounts owing under the Note. This Guarantee remains in effect until the Note is paid in full. Guarantor must pay all amounts due under the Note when Lender makes written demand upon Guarantor. Lender is not required to seek payment from any other source before demanding payment from Guarantor.

2. NOTE:

The "Note" is the promissory note dated _____ June 12, 2017 _____ in the principal amount of ___ Three Hundred Fifty Thousand and no/100 ($350,000.00) ___Dollars,

from Borrower to Lender. It includes any assumption, renewal, substitution, or replacement of the Note, and multiple notes under a line of credit.

3. DEFINITIONS:

"Collateral" means any property taken as security for payment of the Note or any guarantee of the Note.

"Loan" means the loan evidenced by the Note.

"Loan Documents" means the documents related to the Loan signed by Borrower, Guarantor or any other guarantor, or anyone who pledges Collateral.

4. LENDER'S GENERAL POWERS:

Lender may take any of the following actions at any time, without notice, without

Guarantor's consent, and without making demand upon Guarantor:

A. Modify the terms of the Note or any other Loan Document except to increase the amounts due under the Note;

B. Refrain from taking any action on the Note, the Collateral, or any guarantee;

C. Release any Borrower or any guarantor of the Note;

D. Compromise or settle with the Borrower or any guarantor of the Note;

E. Substitute or release any of the Collateral, whether or not Lender receives anything in return;

F. Foreclose upon or otherwise obtain, and dispose of, any Collateral at public or private sale, with or without advertisement;

G. Bid or buy at any sale of Collateral by Lender or any other lienholder, at any price Lender chooses; and

H. Exercise any rights it has, including those in the Note and other Loan Documents.

These actions will not release or reduce the obligations of Guarantor or create any rights or claims against Lender.

5. CHOICE OF LAW:

When Lender is the holder, the Note and this Guarantee will be construed and enforced under New York law. Lender may use state or local procedures for filing papers, recording documents, giving notice, foreclosing liens, and other purposes.

6. RIGHTS, NOTICES, AND DEFENSES THAT GUARANTOR WAIVES:

To the extent permitted by law,

A. Guarantor waives all rights to:

    1) Require presentment, protest, or demand upon Borrower;

    2) Redeem any Collateral before or after Lender disposes of it;

    3) Have any disposition of Collateral advertised; and

    4) Require a valuation of Collateral before or after Lender disposes of it.

B. Guarantor waives any notice of:

    1) Any default under the Note;

    2) Presentment, dishonor, protest, or demand;

    3) Execution of the Note;

    4) Any action or inaction on the Note or Collateral, such as disbursements, payment, nonpayment, acceleration, intent to accelerate, assignment, collection activity, and incurring enforcement expenses;

    5) Any change in the financial condition or business operations of Borrower or any guarantor;

    6) Any changes in the terms of the Note or other Loan Documents, except increases in the amounts due under the Note; and

    7) The time or place of any sale or other disposition of Collateral.

C. Guarantor waives defenses based upon any claim that:

    1) Lender failed to obtain any guaranty;

2) Lender failed to obtain, perfect, or maintain a security interest in any property offered or taken as Collateral;

3) Lender or others improperly valued or inspected the Collateral;

4) The Collateral changed in value, or was neglected, lost, destroyed, or underinsured;

5) Lender impaired the Collateral;

6) Lender did not dispose of any of the Collateral;

7) Lender did not conduct a commercially reasonable sale;

8) Lender did not obtain the fair market value of the Collateral;

9) Lender did not make or perfect a claim upon the death or disability of Borrower or any guarantor of the Note;

10) The financial condition of Borrower or any guarantor was overstated or has adversely changed;

11) Lender made errors or omissions in Loan Documents or administration of the Loan;

12) Lender did not seek payment from the Borrower, any other guarantors, or any Collateral before demanding payment from Guarantor:

13) Lender impaired Guarantor's suretyship rights;

14) Lender modified the Note terms, other than to increase amounts due under the Note. If Lender modifies the Note to increase the amounts due under the Note without Guarantor's consent, Guarantor will not be liable for the increased amounts and related interest and expenses, but remains liable for all other amounts;

15) Borrower has avoided liability on the Note; or

16) Lender has taken an action allowed under the Note, this Guaranty, or other Loan Documents.

7. DUTIES AS TO COLLATERAL:

Guarantor will preserve the Collateral pledged by Guarantor to secure this Guaranty. Lender has no duty to preserve or dispose of any Collateral.

8. SUCCESSORS AND ASSIGNS:

Under this Guaranty, Guarantor includes heirs and successors, and Lender includes its successors and assigns.

9. GENERAL PROVISIONS:

A. ENFORCEMENT EXPENSES. Guarantor promises to pay all expenses that Lender incurs to enforce this Guarantee, including, but not limited to, attorney's fees and costs.

B. SUBROGATION RIGHTS. Guarantor has no subrogation rights as to the Note or the Collateral until the Note is paid in full.

C. JOINT AND SEVERAL LIABILITY. All individuals and entities signing as Guarantor are jointly and severally liable.

D. DOCUMENT SIGNING. Guarantor must sign all documents necessary at any time to comply with the Loan Documents and to enable Lender to acquire, perfect, or maintain Lender's liens on Collateral.

E. FINANCIAL STATEMENTS. Guarantor must give Lender financial statements as Lender requires.

F. LENDER'S RIGHTS CUMULATIVE NOT WAIVED. Lender may exercise any of its rights separately or together, as many times as it chooses. Lender may delay or forgo enforcing any of its rights without losing or impairing any of them.

G. ORAL STATEMENTS NOT BINDING. Guarantor may not use an oral statement to contradict or alter the written terms of the Note or this Guaranty, or to raise a defense to this Guaranty.

H. SEVERABILITY. If any part of this Guaranty is found to be unenforceable, all other parts will remain in effect.

I. CONSIDERATION. The consideration for this Guaranty is the Loan or any accommodation by Lender as to the Loan.

10. GUARANTOR ACKNOWLEDGMENT OF TERMS:

Guarantor acknowledges that Guarantor has read and understands the significance of all terms of the Note and this Guaranty, including all waivers.

11. GUARANTOR NAME(S) AND SIGNATURE(S):

By signing below, each individual or entity becomes obligated as Guarantor under this Guaranty.

WITNESS: GUARANTOR:

_____   _____

ACKNOWLEDGMENT

NEW YORK, ss:

I Hereby Certify, that on this 12th day of June, 2017, before me, the subscriber, a Notary Public of New York, personally appeared Patricia Bouvier, known to me or satisfactorily proven to be the person whose name is subscribed to the within instrument and acknowledged that she executed the same for the purposes therein contained.

AS WITNESS my hand and notarial seal.

_____(SEAL)

Notary Public

My commission Expires: _____

Professional Ethics
in Negotiation & Drafting
Skill: Balance Duties of Client Confidentiality & Honesty

Overview

THIS EXERCISE explores professional ethics associated with negotiating and drafting agreements. It adds some facts to the hypothetical concerning Bianca Bolt's personal guaranty of the obligations of Bolt's Urban Hardware, to First National Bank that require you as attorneys for Bianca and FNB to identify ethical constraints and potential resolutions of competing ethical obligations.

Assume for purposes of this exercise that the lawyers plan to meet prior to the closing of this transaction, when the parties will sign the note, security agreement, and personal guaranty. You and the other lawyer have exchanged drafts of the documents a number of times and believe that you have finalized each document. However, to be sure you have scheduled a brief meeting to ensure that no issues remain to be resolved before the closing.

Unlike the other exercises in this book, this exercise does not require you to produce a written assignment. Instead, you will consider and discuss how to resolve ethical issues that arise during the transaction's finalization. These readings provide the necessary information for that exercise. Part I briefly describes drafters' ethical constraints. Part II recaps the legal rules dictating those obligations, first the relevant ABA Model Rules of Professional Conduct and then cases applying them to common situations. Finally, Part III brings it all together as you review client instructions that add facts to the hypothetical, meet with opposing counsel, and discuss possible ways to balance competing ethical obligations.

Part I: Ethical Obligations in Drafting Explained[1]

Legal drafters are subject to the same ethical rules that govern the conduct of all lawyers. The discussion below is based generally on the ABA Model Rules of Professional Conduct, which have been adopted in most jurisdictions, with some variations and differences of opinion about meaning. This chapter focuses on identifying common ethical problems for drafters and providing general answers, rather than on precise resolutions for each issue.

Concrete answers would be difficult to ascertain. Most of the ethical standards address dilemmas from the perspective of the lawyer as an advocate and the profession has not paid special attention to the ethical problems associated with drafting. Consequently, the legal drafter has less formal guidance from of ethics opinions and court decisions than other lawyers and must rely more on an internal ethical compass. Points on that compass include competence and diligence, following client instructions, avoiding criminal, fraudulent, or other unlawful words and actions, keeping client confidences, loyalty, and calculating legal fees honestly and fairly. We address each in turn.

A. Competence & Diligence

The closely-related duties of competence and diligence rank among the lawyer's highest ethical duties. Mistakes often occur because the lawyer did not know any better or was too lazy or time-crunched to become better informed. Whenever a drafted document fails to produce the results that the client expected, the client is likely to question the competence and diligence of the drafter. A drafter who has been incompetent or lacked diligence has committed an ethical violation and may also face liability for professional malpractice.

---

1   Based on Thomas Haggard & George Kuney, *Legal Drafting*: 89–98 (2d ed. 2007).

Drafting incompetence and lack of diligence include the following:

- Giving a client a set of standard forms and instructions on how to fill them out, when the forms did not actually meet the needs of the client.

- Creating a Clifford Trust that fails to provide the client with the desired tax benefits.[2]

- Failing to include the agreed upon one-year term in an employment contract, thus allowing the client/employee to be terminated before a year expired.

- Drafting a contract that violated the state usury law, which exposes a client to liability.

- Failing to provide properly for a will's intended beneficiaries, thus creating liability to a third party.

- Drafting a contract containing an ambiguity that was later resolved against the client in litigation.

- Failing to obtain, in a timely fashion, a necessary signature on a mortgage, which allowed buyers to sell free and clear of the client's interest in the property.

While the purpose of this book is to train you in competent drafting—which includes assiduous proofreading—you must cultivate other aspects of professional diligence on your own.

---

2   Clifford trusts, usually created on behalf of a minor child, allow income on the principal to be taxed at the child's tax rate, but only if it lasts for a specific period.

B. Follow Client Instructions

A lawyer is bound by the client's decisions about the objectives of the representation—unless they are criminal or fraudulent—but have more discretion regarding the means for achieving them.

Objectives and Means

The critical first step in the drafting process is to determine the client's objectives. Drafters who think that these objectives are not in their client's best interests or are of questionable legality should discuss the matter with the client. This task may be particularly troublesome when the drafter represents an organization. In some instances, the drafter may have to go over the head of the designated organizational representative and present his concerns to higher authority.

Depending on the nature of the relationship, drafters may also discuss with their clients the broader moral, economic, social, and political implications of a given objective. A good lawyer helps clients realize that self-interest is often consistent with decency and social responsibility.

If the client is dedicated to achieving an objective that is deeply and morally offensive to the drafter, then withdrawal is the appropriate response. But drafters must not surreptitiously subvert their clients' objectives or substitute the drafters' objectives for the clients' views. When considering the appropriate response in an ethical quandary, keep in mind the many obstacles—independent of ethical concerns—that stand in the way of withdrawing from a representation that brings in thousands, or even millions, in fees to a firm.

Drafters have more discretion and responsibility in selecting the most effective means of achieving the client's objective. Indeed, many clients leave that up to their lawyers. If, however, the client wants a transaction structured in a way that is not the best way to achieve the ultimate objective, then the drafter should discuss the matter with the client instead of ignoring the client's wishes.

C. Steer Clear of Crimes, Fraud, and Other Illegality

The drafter who correctly advises a client that a transaction violates the law and who later drafts the necessary papers is liable as an accomplice or conspirator. A drafter could not, for example, draft a contract of sale for goods known to be stolen. The "mere scrivener" defense was rejected centuries ago.[3] Similarly, drafter participation in fraud may render the drafter liable for damages to the injured parties, though the courts are divided over some aspects of third-party liability.

A more unsettled area of the law relates to drafter involvement with transaction documents that are neither criminal nor fraudulent, but that are otherwise unlawful, unenforceable, or a sham. For example, a business client might ask a lawyer to draft a covenant-not-to-compete that is geographically overbroad, hoping that the employee will not realize its unenforceability and will unwittingly comply with its limitations. Similarly, the strategic use of *in terrorem*[4] provisions that are either unconscionable or contrary to public policy can be unethical, especially when the parties lack equal bargaining power and the weaker party is not represented by counsel. Finally, a drafter might be asked to draft sham documents that are designed to circumvent some legal limit, such as a sale and resale arrangement in which the alleged profit is actually usurious interest. In these cases the weaker party is duped or intimidated into compliance.

A drafter may not know whether a particular provision is criminal, fraudulent, or otherwise illegal. The law is rife with uncertainty, so good faith predictions are often wrong. The lawyer who makes a good

3   Gregory M. Duhl, "The Ethics of Contract Drafting," 14 *Lewis & Clark L Rev* 989, 1001–1002 (2010).

4   *In terrorem* clauses provide that a party who contests the validity of an agreement forfeits the right to benefit from the contract.

faith prediction and drafts documents on that basis, is generally not deemed unethical. A large gray area lies between the two extremes of a good faith prediction that proves to be inaccurate and conduct that is clearly illegal. For example, would it be unethical for a drafter to state, "I honestly think this provision violates the law, but I can certainly make arguments to the contrary if the issue is litigated," and then proceed to draft the document? The legal ethical community takes a range of views about that lawyer's approach.

Fraud is a particularly slippery concept. A client may ask his attorney to draft a contract containing a term that is so indefinite that it will probably cause the contract to fail. Imagine that your client intends to use this as an escape valve if performance under the contract later becomes unprofitable. Does that constitute fraud against the other party?

Disclosure situations are also troublesome, both legally and ethically. The classic example is the purchaser who contracts to buy a piece of land, knowing that it contains buried treasure, a fact about which the current owner is ignorant. Compare that with the seller of property who contracts to sell without disclosing a latent defect to the buyer. Can the lawyer act as a drafter without insisting that the client disclose the information to the other party?

The drafter's duty of disclosure is fairly clear when mistakes find their way into the final written and signed version of a contract. If the parties have reached an agreement and the lawyer for one of them is responsible for reducing the agreement to writing, that lawyer cannot intentionally and surreptitiously change the terms knowing that the other party is not going to catch it before signing. Moreover, if the later-discovered change or omission that favors the drafter's client was inadvertent, then the drafter should bring the matter to the attention of the other party and may probably do so without first consulting with his or her own client.

Conversely, if an inadvertent clerical or mathematical error favors the non-drafting party, courts generally use doctrines like unilateral mistake to prevent that party from snatching up the advantage. Lawyers should not advise their clients to attempt this kind of subterfuge.

D. Communication & Client Confidentiality

Lawyers are ethically obliged to communicate with their clients and also to keep those communications confidential.

1. Communication

Lawyers must keep their clients reasonably informed about the progress of the representation and provide sufficient explanations to enable them to make informed decisions. These obligations affect both negotiation and drafting stages of a transaction.

First, drafters who also function as negotiators should keep their clients apprised of the status of the negotiations, the content of the counter-proposals, and the concessions that the drafter thinks are appropriate.

Second, lawyers who draft legally complex documents should carefully explain to the client the document's terms and their legal significance.

2. Confidentiality

Professional ethics require confidentiality, a duty to protect client communications from disclosure. It shapes the relationship between attorneys and clients and also formal proceedings by carving out exceptions for disclosure obligations through the evidentiary rule known as the attorney-client privilege.

a. Non-Disclosure

The ethical rules all impose, to some extent, a duty of to protect the client's confidences and secrets. For example, attorneys who draft private documents often obtain personal information about individual clients and their families as well as commercially sensitive and trade secret information from business clients. A lawyer could breach the duty of confidentiality directly or indirectly through office staff. A separation agreement between two movie stars, for example, might well contain many titillating, newsworthy tidbits of information. Confidential business information may also be leaked in this fashion, usually to the substantial financial benefit of the person possessing the information. The drafter must educate secretaries, paralegals, and even couriers about the duty of confidentiality. Make sure to shred drafts of documents that contain sensitive or confidential information, instead of merely putting them in a trash can or recycling bin.

Not disclosing client information to third parties is only part of the ethical duty. The drafter's own use of the information is also limited. For example, the drafter of corporate documents may not use the information when buying or selling stock in the company. That type of insider trading breaches the canons of ethics and may also violate state and federal securities law.

b. Attorney-Client Privilege

The duty of confidentiality also manifests itself in the form of an evidentiary privilege. In essence, a person who seeks legal advice or assistance from a lawyer may invoke an unqualified privilege not to testify about the contents of confidential communications with the lawyer. If asked to testify, the lawyer must also invoke the privilege on behalf of the client.

The privilege probably attaches to most of the information that an attorney obtains when preparing to draft a document. Oddly enough, however, the document itself is not generally privileged unless it contains information that would be privileged. The work-product privilege also arises only in the unlikely circumstance of the document being prepared in anticipation of litigation.

The attorney-client privilege is subject to a number of exceptions that relate to drafters:

i. *Friendly or Business Advice.* The privilege only applies when the lawyer is dealing with drafted documents in the capacity of a lawyer, not situations such as a corporate officer, a business advisor, or a friend.

ii. *Mere Scrivener.* The privilege does not apply to lawyers who have limited roles in drafting routine documents like deeds by acting on the instructions of a client and not giving any legal advice in connection with the drafting. This role is sometimes known as a "mere scrivener." But the scope of this exception is unclear, since drafting even routine documents requires some degree of expertise, even if it is nothing more than knowing that a routine document will indeed suffice. Courts recognize the mere scrivener exception most often when the document is now unavailable and the drafter testifies merely to establish that the document existed and what it contained.

iii. *Third Party Information.* For information to be privileged, it must come from the client, not third parties. This exception comes up most often in the corporate context, where the precise identity of the client is subject to considerable debate.

iv. *Pre-Representation Materials.* The privilege does not apply to otherwise unprivileged client papers that substantially predate the relationship, even if they are given to the drafter for use in drafting a document that will cure whatever legal difficulty the papers present.

v. *Co-Client Information.* When a lawyer is drafting a document for co-clients, information received from one client generally is not privileged from the other client(s). That limit provides another reason to decline requests to draft contracts on behalf of all the contracting parties.

vi. *Fraud and Illegality.* The privilege does not attach to information indicating a client's intent to engage in illegal or fraudulent conduct. This exception would apply if the client gives the drafter information and asks him to draft a document for a fraudulent transaction.

Though these exceptions seem wide-ranging, attorneys generally err on the side of protecting client confidences whenever possible rather than plan on asserting an exception that allows the disclosure.

3. Legal Fees

Ethical rules generally require that the lawyer's fee be reasonable. Reasonableness, in turn, depends on factors such as the time and labor required, the novelty and difficulty of the representation, and the degree of skill that is required. But ethical rules also generally allow the fee amount to reflect the experience and reputation of the lawyer.

Sometimes, these two criteria may work against each other. Consider the lawyer who specializes in wills and estates. Over the years, through "from scratch" drafting of many estate planning documents, the lawyer has crafted provisions dealing with every possible contingency. These provisions are now incorporated into a computerized document assembly program. Basically, all the lawyer does now is obtain the necessary information from new clients, choose the appropriate previously drafted provisions, and merge the two. The time and labor involved in producing that specific document is minimal; but it reflects an enormous amount of experience, reputation, and ability on the part of the lawyer. Clearly, the drafter cannot bill for fictitious hours. The drafter may, however, adopt an approach known as "value billing" for a set fee instead of by the hour.

Drafters face a similar problem when they use essentially the same document for multiple clients. For example, a lawyer may draft a from-scratch document for a client, at $100 per hour for ten hours, or $1,000. A few weeks later, another client needs an almost identical document. Now it takes the lawyer only an hour to produce it. Must the drafter charge only $100? Can the drafter charge another $1,000? Or is the correct fee somewhere in between? Again, the lawyer cannot bill the second client at a fictitious hourly rate, but he may charge a flat fee for the document that is in excess of the normal hourly rate, as long as the client agrees to value billing in advance.

4. Conflicts of Interest

The touchstone of drafting ethics is that the contract drafter acts on behalf of a client. The contract drafter usually drafts on behalf of only one of the contracting parties because lawyers have a duty of unqualified loyalty to their clients. That duty cannot be fulfilled if the attorney attempts to represent two clients with adverse interests. Certainly, an attorney could not represent the plaintiff and also the defendant in a tort action, given the conflict of interests.

The parties to a contract have adverse or conflicting interests with respect to the specific terms of that exchange, even though exchange will not be finalized unless it is mutually beneficial. A skillful and conscientious drafter who represents a seller will draft terms that benefit the seller, and one acting on behalf of a buyer would similarly represent that client. It is thus difficult, if not impossible, for the same lawyer to represent both buyer and seller. Indeed, the only situations in which joint representation would be permissible involve very simple transactions, where the parties have already reached an agreement and the lawyer's only task is to reduce that agreement to writing. But even here the lawyer must be satisfied that the terms are compatible with the best interest of both parties and that he can be impartial as she drafts. If, after reviewing the terms of the agreement, the lawyer determines that the contract will not be fair to one of the parties, the lawyer must decline to draft the document and suggest that both parties retain separate attorneys to advise them on the matter.

Having described the main ethical concepts that shape the conduct of transactional lawyers—which also apply to litigators and others who negotiate and draft settlement agreements—it is time to review the text of those rules themselves.

Part II: Legal Rules Explained

Ethical obligations are defined by each state in both Ethical Rules and opinions of the bar association that apply the Rules to a particular situation. We address in turn.

A. Rules of Professional Conduct[5]

The Model Rules of Professional Conduct govern various aspects of a lawyer's relationships with clients, courts and other adjudicative or regulatory bodies, the bar, and the general public. The Rules below are organized in three areas of a lawyer's professional life: interactions with clients; interactions with everyone else, from opposing counsel to the

---

5   © 2016 by the American Bar Association. Reprinted with permission. All rights reserved. This information or any or portion thereof may not be copied or disseminated in any form or by any means or stored in an electronic database or retrieval system without the express written consent of the American Bar Association. Copies of ABA Model Rules of Professional Conduct are available at "http://shop.aba.org/" http://shopABA.org.

general public; and the lawyer's duty to maintain the integrity of the profession.

1. Client-Lawyer Relationship

Rule 1.2 Scope of Representation and Allocation of Authority between Client and Lawyer

(a) Subject to paragraphs (c) and (d), a lawyer shall abide by a client's decisions concerning the objectives of representation and, as required by Rule 1.4, shall consult with the client as to the means by which they are to be pursued. A lawyer may take such action on behalf of the client as is impliedly authorized to carry out the representation. A lawyer shall abide by a client's decision whether to settle a matter. In a criminal case, the lawyer shall abide by the client's decision, after consultation with the lawyer, as to a plea to be entered, whether to waive jury trial and whether the client will testify.

(b) A lawyer's representation of a client, including representation by appointment, does not constitute an endorsement of the client's political, economic, social or moral views or activities.

(c) A lawyer may limit the scope of the representation if the limitation is reasonable under the circumstances and the client gives informed consent.

(d) A lawyer shall not counsel a client to engage, or assist a client, in conduct that the lawyer knows is criminal or fraudulent, but a lawyer may discuss the legal consequences of any proposed course of conduct with a client and may counsel or assist a client to make a good faith effort to determine the validity, scope, meaning or application of the law.

Rule 1.4 Communication

(a)   A lawyer shall:

    (1) promptly inform the client of any decision or circumstance with respect to which the client's informed consent, as defined in Rule 1.0(e), is required by these Rules;

    (2) reasonably consult with the client about the means by which the client's objectives are to be accomplished;

    (3) keep the client reasonably informed about the status of the matter;

    (4) promptly comply with reasonable requests for information; and

    (5) consult with the client about any relevant limitation on the lawyer's conduct when the lawyer knows that the client expects assistance not permitted by the Rules of Professional Conduct or other law.

(b)   A lawyer shall explain a matter to the extent reasonably necessary to permit the client to make informed decisions regarding the representation.

Rule 1.6 Confidentiality of Information

(a) A lawyer shall not reveal information relating to the representation of a client unless the client gives informed consent, the disclosure is impliedly authorized in order to carry out the representation or the disclosure is permitted by paragraph (b).

(b) A lawyer may reveal information relating to the representation of a client to the extent the lawyer reasonably believes necessary:

(1) to prevent reasonably certain death or substantial bodily harm;

(2) to prevent the client from committing a crime or fraud that is reasonably certain to result in substantial injury to the financial interests or property of another and in furtherance of which the client has used or is using the lawyer's services;

(3) to prevent, mitigate or rectify substantial injury to the financial interests or property of another that is reasonably certain to result or has resulted from the client's commission of a crime or fraud in furtherance of which the client has used the lawyer's services;

(4) to secure legal advice about the lawyer's compliance with these Rules;

(5) to establish a claim or defense on behalf of the lawyer in a controversy between the lawyer and the client, to establish a defense to a criminal charge or civil claim against the lawyer based upon conduct in which the client was involved, or to respond to allegations in any proceeding concerning the lawyer's representation of the client;

(6) to comply with other law or a court order; or

(7) to detect and resolve conflicts of interest arising from the lawyer's change of employment or from changes in the composition or ownership of a firm, but only if the revealed information would not compromise the attorney-client privilege or otherwise prejudice the client.

(c) A lawyer shall make reasonable efforts to prevent the inadvertent or unauthorized disclosure of, or unauthorized access to, information relating to the representation of a client.

Rule 2.1 Advisor

In representing a client, a lawyer shall exercise independent professional judgment and render candid advice. In rendering advice, a lawyer may refer not only to law but to other considerations such as moral, economic, social and political factors, which may be relevant to the client's situation.

2. Transactions with Persons Other than Clients

Rule 4.1 Truthfulness in Statements to Others

In the course of representing a client a lawyer shall not knowingly:

(a) make a false statement of material fact or law to a third person; or

(b) fail to disclose a material fact to a third person when disclosure is necessary to avoid assisting a criminal or fraudulent act by a client, unless disclosure is prohibited by Rule 1.6.

Rule 4.4 Respect for Rights of Third Persons

(a) In representing a client, a lawyer shall not use means that have no substantial purpose other than to embarrass, delay, or burden a third person, or use methods of obtaining evidence that violate the legal rights of such a person.

(b) A lawyer who receives a document or electronically stored information relating to the representation of the lawyer's client and knows or reasonably should know that the document or electronically stored information was inadvertently sent shall promptly notify the sender.

3. Maintaining the Integrity of the Profession

Rule 8.4 Misconduct

It is professional misconduct for a lawyer to:

(a) violate or attempt to violate the Rules of Professional Conduct, knowingly assist or induce another to do so, or do so through the acts of another;

(b) commit a criminal act that reflects adversely on the lawyer's honesty, trustworthiness or fitness as a lawyer in other respects;

(c) engage in conduct involving dishonesty, fraud, deceit or misrepresentation;

(d) engage in conduct that is prejudicial to the administration of justice;

(e) state or imply an ability to influence improperly a government agency or official or to achieve results by means that violate the Rules of Professional Conduct or other law; or

(f) knowingly assist a judge or judicial officer in conduct that is a violation of applicable rules of judicial conduct or other law.

B. Case Law & Opinions on Unethical Practices

Attorneys are governed by the Bar Associations of the state in which they practice, so ethical duties can vary across jurisdictions. Moreover, as noted earlier in this chapter, most cases or advisory opinions involve situations that arise during litigation instead of transactional work. The following cases represent a sample of case law and advisory opinions that provide guidance to lawyers as they negotiate and draft agreements.

1. Duty to Disclose

In the Matter of Robert J. CANTRELL, Respondent.
619 S.E.2d 434 (SC 2005)

Opinion

PER CURIAM:

In this attorney disciplinary matter, respondent and the Office of Disciplinary Counsel (ODC) have entered into an Agreement for Discipline by Consent pursuant to Rule 21, RLDE, Rule 413, SCACR[6]. In the Agreement, respondent admits misconduct and consents to the imposition of a two year suspension from the practice of law. We accept the Agreement and impose a two year suspension from the practice of law. The facts, as set forth in the Agreement, are as follows.

[The court describes other instances of respondent failing to communicate with clients, using cocaine, trespassing in a family law case, and practicing law without a license.]

Matter III

On or about October 31, 2002, respondent filed a Chapter 13 bankruptcy action on behalf of a client. Subsequent to the filing, respondent took

---

6   RLDE stands for Rules for Lawyer Disciplinary Enforcement and SCACR stands for South Carolina Appellate Court Rule. [ed].

over representation of the client's ongoing worker's compensation case. On or about January 3, 2003, the bankruptcy trustee filed a Petition to Dismiss the bankruptcy action due to nonpayment.

On or about January 27, 2003, respondent assisted his client in obtaining a loan from the complainant in this matter. The loan was to be repaid through the proceeds of the worker's compensation action. Respondent submitted the loan application to the complainant on behalf of respondent and his client. Respondent failed to notify the complainant of the client's bankruptcy filing at the time he submitted the loan application. Although the client's bankruptcy action was ultimately dismissed, respondent actively assisted his client in obtaining a personal loan without making full disclosure of all relevant financial information.

* * *

Respondent represents that a significant factor during the period of time of his misconduct was his very contentious divorce and custody action with his first wife. Respondent represents that before and/or during this marital discord, he hired an employee as his paralegal and office manager. Respondent admits he allowed this employee to control every aspect of his law office, including but not limited to, relinquishing authority to make decisions regarding the representation of his clients.

LAW

Respondent admits that his misconduct constitutes grounds for discipline under Rule 413, RLDE, specifically Rule 7(a)(1) (lawyer shall not violate Rules of Professional Conduct or any other rules of this jurisdiction regarding professional conduct of lawyers), Rule 7(a)(2) (it shall be a ground for discipline for a lawyer to engage in conduct in violation of the applicable rules of professional conduct of another jurisdiction),

[and] Rule 7(a)(5) (lawyer shall not engage in conduct tending to pollute the administration of justice or to bring the courts or the legal profession into disrepute or conduct demonstrating an unfitness to practice law) . . . . In addition, respondent admits he has violated the following provisions of the Rules of Professional Conduct, Rule 407, SCACR: Rule 1.1 (lawyer shall provide competent representation to a client); Rule 1.3 (lawyer shall act with reasonable diligence and promptness in representing a client); Rule 1.4 (lawyer shall keep client reasonably informed about status of a matter and promptly comply with reasonable requests for information); . . . Rule 3.2 (lawyer shall make reasonable efforts to expedite litigation consistent with interests of the client); . . . Rule 4.1 (in the course of representing a client, a lawyer shall not fail to disclose a material fact to a third person when disclosure is necessary to avoid assisting a fraudulent act by a client); Rule 5.5 (lawyer shall not practice law in a jurisdiction where doing so violates the regulation of the legal profession in that jurisdiction); Rule 8.1 (lawyer shall not knowingly fail to respond to a lawful demand for information from a disciplinary authority); Rule 8.4(a) (lawyer shall not violate the Rules of Professional Conduct); . . . Rule 8.4(c) (it shall be professional misconduct for a lawyer to engage in conduct involving moral turpitude); Rule 8.4(d) (lawyer shall not engage in conduct involving dishonesty, fraud, deceit, or misrepresentation); and Rule 8.4(e) (lawyer shall not engage in conduct that is prejudicial to administration of justice).

CONCLUSION

We accept the Agreement for Discipline by Consent and impose a two year definite suspension from the practice of law. During the suspension, respondent shall continue to participate in any counseling and/or treatment recommended by his psychologist. Respondent's psychologist shall submit quarterly evaluations of respondent's progress to ODC throughout the duration of the suspension. In addition, if respondent seeks reinstatement to the practice of law, he shall submit a report from his psychologist to ODC which addresses his mental fitness to resume the practice of law. This report shall be submitted to ODC at least sixty (60) days prior to filing any petition for reinstatement. Respondent's request that the suspension be applied retroactively to the date of his interim suspension is denied. Within fifteen days of the date of this opinion, respondent shall file an affidavit with the Clerk of Court showing that he has complied with Rule 30, RLDE, Rule 413, SCACR.

DEFINITE SUSPENSION.

TOAL, C.J., MOORE, WALLER, BURNETT and PLEICONES, JJ., concur.

2. Scrivener's Error

Drafters refer to typos as "scrivener's errors." As the case below explains, professional ethics preclude attorneys from taking advantage of this kind of error by the other side, even if a client instructs them to.

Advisory Opinion 1987-11
State bar of New Mexico[7]
Ethics Advisory Committee

An attorney asks whether he has an obligation to disclose to the opposing party its apparent error under the following circumstances. The attorney represents the plaintiff in a personal injury case.

---

7   Available at http://www.nmbar.org/NmbarDocs/AboutUs/committees/Ethics/1987/1987-11.pdf
Reprinted with permission. The advisory opinions on the website are a historical record of the committee and an opinion may be currently out-of-date or otherwise no longer applicable with regards to our current Rules of Professional Conduct.

Prior to filing suit, the attorney attempted to settle with the insurance company. The attorney demanded $20,000. The company was willing to settle for $1,000. The attorney countered with a proposal for $10,000. The company countered with its own proposal for $1,400. The attorney wrote the company a letter, threatening suit unless the matter were settled for $10,000.

The company tendered him a check for $14,000 in settlement of the matter. It is the opinion of the committee that the attorney should disclose to the company its apparent error.

The ABA Committee on Ethics and Professional Responsibility recently addressed a similar question. In ABA Informal opinion 86-1518, the committee opined that a client does not have a right to take unfair advantage of a scrivener's error in omitting an important provision from a contract. Based on the facts of this attorney's case, it is obvious that the insurance company erroneously tendered a check with an extra zero. While we do not condone the insurance company's tactic of tendering a check in settlement for an amount which the client has already rejected (perhaps hoping that the client would endorse the check in error), we do not believe that this permits the attorney to engage in similar dishonorable behavior. Knowing that the check was mistakenly tendered, we believe that the attorney's duty is to act with honesty and to avoid a possible fraud.

3. Conflicting Obligations: Compliance with Client Instructions, Honesty & Confidentiality

The following case combines several issues: following client instructions, refraining from fraud and misrepresentation, and keeping attorney-client confidences.

Formal Opinion Number. 2013-189
CA Eth. Op. 2013-189, 2013 WL 3505630
California State Bar
Standing Committee on
Professional Responsibility and Conduct[8]

STATEMENT OF FACTS

Buyer and Seller have been in discussions regarding the sale of the Company from Seller to Buyer, and have agreed in concept to some of the material terms, including total consideration of $5 million to be paid by Buyer and Buyer's requirement that Seller enter into a covenant not to compete with the Company following the sale. Buyer's Attorney and Seller's Attorney are tasked with preparing a Purchase and Sale Agreement to reflect the agreement of the parties.

Buyer's Attorney prepares an initial draft of the Purchase and Sale Agreement. One section towards the back of the 50-page draft agreement contains the terms of an enforceable covenant not to compete, and includes a provision that Buyer's sole and exclusive remedy for a breach by Seller of its covenant not to compete is the return of that portion of the total consideration which has been allocated in the Purchase and Sale Agreement for the covenant not to compete. Another section in the front of the draft agreement provides that, of the $5 million to be paid by Buyer, $3 million is to be allocated to the purchase price for the Company and $2 million is to be allocated as consideration for the covenant not to compete.

Scenario A

After soliciting input on the initial draft from Seller and Seller's tax advisor, Seller's Attorney provides Buyer's Attorney with comments on the initial draft, including the observation from Seller's tax advisor that payments received by Seller with respect to the covenant not to compete are not as favorable, from a tax perspective, as payments with respect to the purchase price for the Company.

Buyer's Attorney then prepares a revised version of the Purchase and Sale Agreement which, apparently in response to the comments of Seller's Attorney, provides for an allocation of only $1 as consideration for the covenant not to compete with $4,999,999 allocated to the purchase price for the Company. In reviewing the changes made in the revised version, Seller's Attorney recognizes that the allocation of only $1 as consideration for the covenant not to compete essentially renders the covenant meaningless, because Buyer's sole and exclusive remedy for breach by Seller of the covenant would be the return by Seller of $1 of the total consideration. Seller's Attorney notifies Seller about the apparent error with respect to the consequences of the change made by Buyer's Attorney. Seller instructs Seller's Attorney to not inform Buyer's Attorney of this apparent error. Seller's Attorney says nothing to Buyer's Attorney and allows the Purchase and Sale Agreement to be entered into by the parties in that form.

Scenario B

After receiving the initial draft from Buyer's Attorney, Seller's Attorney prepares a revised version of the Purchase and Sale Agreement which provides for an allocation of only $1 as consideration for the covenant not to compete, with the intent of essentially rendering the covenant not to compete meaningless. Although Seller's Attorney had no intention of keeping this change secret from Buyer's Attorney, Seller's Attorney generates a "redline" of the draft that unintentionally failed to highlight the change, and then tenders the revised version to Buyer's Attorney. Subsequently, Seller's Attorney discovers the unintended defect in the "redline" and notifies Seller about the change, including the failure to highlight the change, in the revised version. Seller instructs Seller's Attorney to not inform Buyer's Attorney of the change. Seller's Attorney says nothing to Buyer's Attorney and allows the Purchase and Sale Agreement to be entered into by the parties in that form.

Under either Scenario, has Seller's Attorney violated any ethical duties?

DISCUSSION

Following Client's Instruction to Not Disclose

Attorneys generally must follow the instructions of their clients. See ABA Model Rule 1.2(a).[9] However, if the client insists on certain unethical conduct, the attorney may have an obligation to withdraw from the representation.... Such an obligation, for example, may arise if the unethical conduct in question involves a fraudulent failure to make a disclosure. As the Los Angeles County Bar Association has opined, upon discovering that an adverse party made an overpayment under a settlement agreement,

> [c]ounsel is obligated to inform his/her client of the overpayment under [rule] 3-500.... [W]here the client has requested the information be held in confidence, the attorney is obligated to preserve the secret. The attorney should counsel the client to disclose and return the overpayment. If the client refuses, however, the attorney must consider whether the failure to disclose constitutes fraud. The attorney must then determine whether he/she may or must withdraw from the representation.[10]

---

9   The ABA Model Rules are not binding in California but may be used for guidance by lawyers where there is no direct California authority and the ABA Model Rules do not conflict with California policy.

10   LA Bar Ass'n Formal Op. No. 520.

Under either Scenario A or Scenario B of our Statement of Facts, once Seller's Attorney has informed Seller of the development,[11] Seller's Attorney must abide by the instruction of Seller to not disclose. If, however, failure to make such disclosure constitutes an ethical violation by Seller's Attorney, then Seller's Attorney may have an obligation to withdraw from the representation under such circumstances. See Cal. State Bar Formal Opn. No. 1996-146.

Failure to Alert Opposing Counsel

Attorneys are held to a high standard, and may be subject to general obligations of professionalism. For example, attorneys have been held to have a duty to respect the legitimate interests of opposing counsel. "An attorney has an obligation not only to protect his client's interests but also to respect the legitimate interests of fellow members of the bar, the judiciary, and the administration of justice." *Kirsch v. Duryea*, 146 Cal.Rptr. 218 (1978). Further, this Committee has previously concluded that attorneys should treat opposing counsel with candor and fairness.

Any duty of professionalism, however, is secondary to the duties owed by attorneys to their own clients. There is no general duty to protect the interests of non-clients. Furthermore, a duty to non-clients would damage the attorney-client relationship.

Attorneys generally owe no duties to opposing counsel nor do they have any obligation to correct the mistakes of opposing counsel. There

---

11   Attorneys have an obligation to keep their clients reasonably informed about significant developments relating to the matter for which they have been employed. Both the apparent error made by Buyer's Attorney in Scenario A and the intentional change made by Seller's Attorney in Scenario B would constitute a "'significant development," which would require that Seller be informed of the potential for added costs and burdens of enforcement, including litigation and the likelihood that Buyer may seek reformation of the Purchase and Sale Agreement. On the other hand, if Seller's Attorney intends to inform Buyer's Attorney of the apparent error, Seller's Attorney need not inform Seller of the apparent error. Where a client has already agreed to a contract provision which is inadequately reflected in the draft contract prepared by opposing counsel, the inadvertent error by opposing counsel by itself (i.e., unless left uncorrected in the final executed version) does not constitute a significant development, and the client's attorney may correct the drafting error and need not inform the client. See ABA Informal Opn. No. 86-1518 (attorney has no obligation to inform his client of the error because "the decision on the contract ha[d] already been made by the client.").

is no liability for conscious nondisclosure absent a duty of disclosure. There is also no duty to correct erroneous assumptions of opposing counsel. See ABA Formal Opn. No. 94-387 (no duty to disclose to opposing party that statute of limitations has run).[12]

On the other hand, it is unlawful (and a violation of an attorney's ethical obligations) for an attorney to commit any act of moral turpitude, dishonesty, or corruption. It is similarly inappropriate for an attorney to engage in deceit or active concealment, or [to] make a false statement of a material fact to a non-client. Also, an attorney may not knowingly assist his or her client in any criminal or fraudulent conduct.

As a result, an attorney may have an obligation to inform opposing counsel of his or her error if and to the extent that failure to do so would constitute fraud, a material misstatement, or engaging in misleading or deceitful conduct. Accordingly, a lawyer communicating on behalf of a client with a non-client may not knowingly make a false statement of material fact to the non-client. "One who is asked for or volunteers information must be truthful, and the telling of a half-truth calculated to deceive is fraud." *Cicone v. URS Corp.* 183 Cal.App.3d 194, 201 (1986).

Scenario A

In Scenario A of our Statement of Facts, although the Purchase and Sale Agreement contains a covenant not to compete, the apparent error of Buyer's Attorney limits the effectiveness of the covenant because the penalty for breach results in payment by Seller of only $1. However, Seller's Attorney has engaged in no conduct or activity that induced the apparent error. Further, under our Statement of Facts, there had been no agreement on the allocation of the purchase price to the covenant, and

---

12   This opinion does not address a scrivener's error. See ABA Informal Opn. No. 86-1518: interpreting Model Rule 1.2(d) to conclude that where a transcription of an agreement contains a scrivener's error, an attorney cannot allow his or her client to benefit from the mistake and must notify the other party's attorney. But see Md. State Bar Ass'n, Comm. on Ethics Opn. No. 89-44 (1989) (opining that there is no obligation to reveal the omission of a material term in a contract).

the Purchase and Sale Agreement does in fact contain a covenant not to compete the terms of which are consistent with the parties' mutual understanding. Under these circumstances, where Seller's Attorney has not engaged in deceit, active concealment or fraud, we conclude that Seller's Attorney does not have an affirmative duty to disclose the apparent error to Buyer's Attorney.

Scenario B

Had Seller's Attorney intentionally created a defective "redline" to surreptitiously conceal the change to the covenant not to compete, his conduct would constitute deceit, active concealment and possibly fraud, in violation of Seller's Attorney's ethical obligations. However, in Scenario B of our Statement of Facts, Seller's Attorney *intentionally* made the change which essentially renders the covenant not to compete meaningless, but *unintentionally* provided a defective "redline" that failed to highlight for Buyer's Attorney that the change had been made. Under these circumstances, and prior to discovery of the unintentional defect, Seller's Attorney has engaged in no such unethical conduct. But once Seller's Attorney realizes his own error, we conclude that the failure to correct that error and advise Buyer's Attorney of the change might be conduct that constitutes deceit, active concealment and/or fraud, with any such determination to be based on the relevant facts and circumstances.[13] If Seller instructs Seller's Attorney to not advise Buyer's Attorney of the change, where failure to do so would be a violation of his ethical obligations, Seller's Attorney may have to consider withdrawing.[14]

---

[13]   Any such determination—which may depend, for example, on whether the changed provision is further negotiated and revised (thereby effectively calling Buyer's Attorney's attention to the changed language)—is beyond the scope of this opinion.

[14]   Subject to any ethical obligations regarding withdrawal from representation. See, e.g., rule 3-700.

CONCLUSION

Where an attorney has engaged in no conduct or activity that induced an apparent material error by opposing counsel, the attorney has no obligation to alert the opposing counsel of the apparent error. However, where the attorney has made a material change in contract language in such a manner that his conduct constitutes deceit, active concealment, or fraud, the failure of the attorney to alert opposing counsel of the change would be a violation of his ethical obligations.

As lawyers and clients communicate more by email, and email is easily forwarded to someone not in the original conversation, it is easy for an attorney to mistakenly share client confidences. Model Rule 4.4 addresses this danger directly and requires the attorney to promptly notify anyone who mistakenly sent information that was supposed to remain confidential. The following advisory opinion clarifies the duty.

Duty When Lawyer Receives Copies of a Third Party's Email Communications with Counsel
ABA Formal Op. 11-460
© American Bar Association[15]
August 4, 2011

This opinion addresses a lawyer's ethical duty upon receiving copies of emails between a third party and the third party's lawyer. We explore this question in the context of the following hypothetical scenario.

After an employee files a lawsuit against her employer, the employer copies the contents of her workplace computer for possible use in defending the lawsuit, and provides copies to its outside counsel. Upon review, the employer's counsel sees that some of the employee's emails bear the legend "Attorney-Client Confidential Communication." Must the employer's counsel notify the employee's lawyer that the employer has accessed this correspondence?

When an employer's lawyer receives copies of an employee's private communications with counsel, which the employer located in the employee's business email file or on the employee's workplace computer or other device, the question arises whether the employer's lawyer must notify opposing counsel pursuant to Rule 4.4(b). This Rule provides: "A lawyer who receives a document relating to the representation of the lawyer's client and knows or reasonably should know that the document was inadvertently sent shall promptly notify the sender."

Rule 4.4(b) does not expressly address this situation, because emails between an employee and his or her counsel are not "inadvertently sent" by either of them. A "document [is] inadvertently sent" to someone when it is accidentally transmitted to an unintended recipient, as occurs when an email or letter is misaddressed or when a document is accidentally attached to an email or accidentally included among other documents produced in discovery. But a document is not "inadvertently sent" when it is retrieved by a third person from a public or private place where it is stored or left.

The question remains whether Rule 4.4(b) implicitly addresses this situation. In several cases, courts have found that Rule 4.4(b) or its underlying principle requires disclosure in analogous situations, such as when "confidential documents are sent intentionally and without permission." *Chamberlain Group, Inc. v. Lear Corp.*, 270 F.R.D. 392, 398 (N.D. Ill. 2010). In *Stengart v. Loving Care Agency, Inc.*, 990 A.2d 650, 665 (N.J. 2010), the court found that the employer's lawyer in an employment litigation violated the state's version of Rule 4.4(b) by failing to notify the employee's counsel that the employer had downloaded and intended to use copies of pre-suit email messages exchanged between the employee and her lawyers.

Since Rule 4.4(b) was added to the Model Rules, this Committee twice has declined to interpret it or other rules to require notice to opposing counsel other than in the situation that Rule 4.4(b) expressly addresses. In ABA Formal Op. 06-442 (2006), we considered whether a lawyer could properly review and use information embedded in electronic documents (i.e., metadata) received from opposing counsel or an adverse party. We concluded, contrary to some other bar association ethics committees, that the Rule did not apply. We reasoned that "the recent addition of Rule 4.4(b) identifying the sole requirement of providing notice to the sender of the receipt of inadvertently sent information [was] evidence of the intention to set no other specific restrictions on the receiving lawyer's conduct." Likewise, in ABA Formal Op. 06-440, this Committee found that Rule 4.4(b) does not obligate a lawyer to notify opposing counsel that the lawyer has received privileged or otherwise confidential materials of the adverse party from someone who was not authorized to provide the materials, if the materials were not provided as "the result of the sender's inadvertence." We noted that other law might prevent the receiving lawyer from retaining and using the materials, and that the lawyer might be subject to sanction for doing so, but concluded that this was "a matter of law beyond the scope of Rule 4.4(b)."

To say that Rule 4.4(b) and other rules are inapplicable is not to say that courts cannot or should not impose a disclosure obligation in this context pursuant to their supervisory or other authority. As Comment [2] to Rule 4.4(b) observes, "this Rule does not address the legal duties of a lawyer who receives a document that the lawyer knows or reasonably should know may have been wrongfully obtained by the sending person." Pursuant to their supervisory authority, courts may require lawyers in litigation to notify the opposing counsel when their clients provide an opposing party's attorney-client confidential communications that were retrieved from a computer or other device owned or possessed by the client. Alternatively, the civil procedure rules governing discovery in the litigation may require the employer to notify the employee that it has gained possession of the employee's attorney-client communications. Insofar as courts recognize a legal duty in this situation, as the court in *Stengart* has done, a lawyer may be subject to discipline, not just litigation sanction, for knowingly violating it. However, the Model Rules do not independently impose an ethical duty to notify opposing counsel of the receipt of private, potentially privileged email communications between the opposing party and his or her counsel.

When the law governing potential disclosure is unclear, the lawyer need not risk violating a legal or ethical obligation. The fact that the employer-client has obtained copies of the employee's emails is "information relating to the representation of [the] client" that must be kept confidential under Rule 1.6(a) unless there is an applicable exception to the confidentiality obligation or the client gives "informed consent" to disclosure. Rule 1.6(b)(6) permits a lawyer to "reveal information relating to the representation of a client to the extent the lawyer reasonably believes necessary . . . to comply with other law or a court order." Rule 1.6(b)(6) allows the employer's lawyer to disclose that the employer has retrieved the employee's attorney-client email communications to the extent he or she reasonably believes it is necessary to do so to comply with the relevant law, even if the legal obligation is not free from doubt. On the other hand, if no law can reasonably be read as establishing a reporting obligation, then the decision whether to give notice must be made by the employer-client. Even when there is no clear notification obligation, it often will be in the employer-client's best interest to give notice and obtain a judicial ruling as to the admissibility of the employee's attorney-client communications before attempting to use them and, if possible, before the employer's lawyer reviews them. This course minimizes the risk of disqualification or other sanction if the court ultimately concludes that the opposing party's communications with counsel are privileged and inadmissible. The employer's lawyer must explain these and other implications of disclosure, and the available alternatives, as necessary to enable the employer to make an informed decision.

Part III: Student Assignment

This assignment has three parts, but no writing requirement.

A. Review Client Instructions

Assume for purposes of this exercise only that your clients have completed negotiations and drafting for the promissory note, financing statement, security agreement, and personal guaranty. Only two steps remain. At the closing next week, the parties and attorneys will convene to sign the documents and for FNB to disburse the funds. Before that, you and the attorney for the other side will meet to make sure that all that is left to do is for the clients to sign the documents.

To prepare for this meeting you have a telephone conversation with your client to make sure that no issues remain to be resolved. Because these communications are privileged, you will know only the communications from your own client. Your professor will provide you with instructions from your client about how to approach the pre-closing meeting with the other side.

After you read these instructions, confer with other students who represent your side of the deal, just as lawyers in an office would confer with one another in a situation like this. Identify the Model Rules and case law implicated by the client instructions and brainstorm how to talk your client out of any ethical behavior. Then select one of you to play the role of opposing counsel.

Use this simulation to imagine what opposing counsel might ask you, and how you might answer. Jot down phrases and ideas as you identify ways to ask and answer questions in the pre-closing meeting that comply with your professional obligations as an attorney.

B. Meet with Opposing Counsel

Hold the pre-closing meeting with your opposing counsel. Stay in role during the meeting. Follow your client's instructions and comply with your ethical obligations.

C. Class Discussion

After the pre-closing meeting, the class will find out what the other side's client instructed and report how their discussion with opposing counsel went. Be prepared to discuss which Rules of Professional Conduct shaped your words and conduct, and how you balanced competing duties, or failed to comply with professional ethics.

At the end, you should be better prepared to navigate this kind of quandary in practice, and have phrases as well as sentence structures that can help a lawyer comply with competing ethical imperatives.

Certificate of Title Goods & Fixtures
Skill: Navigate Multiple Doctrinal Systems

Overview

This exercise builds on the foundational skills developed in earlier chapters in two ways. First, it adds two common doctrinal twists, then it requires you to engage in a strategic analysis of costs and benefits of a lender doing everything possible to be perfected against the greatest number of competitors. On the doctrinal level, statutes other than Article 9 provide special rules for perfection of security interests in particular kinds of collateral, including aircraft, motor vehicles, and goods closely associated with land. But knowing these legal rules gives you only part of the information that clients pay their attorneys to provide. Once you know what a secured party must do to perfect its interest in a motor vehicle or land and how to take those steps, you should also be able to advise a client whether maximum compliance is worth the time, money and trouble.

Assume the following facts for purposes of this exercise only. FNB wants to take a security interest in a truck owned by Bolt's Urban Hardware, LLC ("debtor" or the "Store") and also goods such as display shelves awnings, lighting, and counters that are attached to the real property where the Store is located. These items likely qualify as "fixtures" under Article 9 and real property doctrines. Details about the truck and fixtures are provided in the student assignment below.

Part I of this exercise explains the way that FNB would perfect a security interest in the Store's delivery truck and the fixtures and explores whether FNB's counsel should recommend that the bank take all necessary steps to perfect its security interests in the fixtures. While the other exercises in this book have you play the roles of FNB and the Store's counsel, in this one the student who has played debtor's counsel should act out the part of Lamar Lee, the Vice President at the bank. Part II applies both lessons by having you fill out a Notice of Lien that would perfect a security interest in the Store's truck, and also make sure that your security agreement and financing statement cover fixtures.

Part I: Doctrine Explained Re: Perfection for Motor Vehicles & Fixtures

Secured transactions courses generally cover UCC §§ 9-311's rules that require a secured creditor to comply with federal or state statutes to perfect a security interest in aircraft, a motor vehicle, or other specific types of collateral. The situation that comes up most often—and is already familiar to most people who have bought or sold a car—is a creditor perfecting its security interest in a vehicle by noting a lien on its certificate of title. But few students come out of a commercial law class knowing how this process works. This exercise fills that gap.

Along the same lines, many secured transactions courses only briefly mention collateral that is closely associated with real estate. The rules governing security interests in land differ considerably from state to state and also from Article 9's rules. For the same reasons this book focuses on personal property. But this exercise partly plugs that hole by addressing fixtures, goods which are a hybrid between real and personal property and therefore get hybrid treatment under legal doctrine. Accordingly Section A below shows how to perfect a security interest in motor vehicles, and Section B below explores the two ways that an Article 9 secured creditor can perfect a security interest in fixtures such as awnings, lighting, shelving and other things attached to real estate.

Like most legal systems, Article 9 is made up of general rules and exceptions (as well as occasional exceptions to the exceptions). For example, §9–310 dictates that the general way to perfect a security interest is to file a financing statement in the state files, as you did in exercise #3.[1] But that is just a default rule. If the collateral is a deposit account, UCC §§ 9–312 and 9–314 dictate that a secured creditor perfect its security interest by control, a method described in § 9–104.[2] Along the same lines, money—cash—can only be perfected by possession.[3] This exercise involves two other types of exceptional collateral, first explaining the exception for motor vehicles, and then for fixtures.

Since the transaction between FNB and the Store happens in New York, our discussion focuses on the rules of that state in effect as of late 2016. Your professor may have you comply with your state rules, which may be similar.

A. Perfection in Motor Vehicles

Motor vehicles are an exception to the rule of perfecting-by-filing a financing statement, but the rule also contains an exception to that exception. Recall that the UCC §9–102 classifies collateral based on the debtor's primary use. Inventory is held for sale or lease, while equipment are goods other than inventory, consumer goods or farm products. Article 9 provides a different rule for perfecting a motor vehicle that is inventory from one that is held as equipment or consumer goods.

1. Article 9 Rules

Take a 2015 Toyota Prius. If that Prius is held by a debtor who uses it in her business as a real estate broker, then UCC§§ 9–311(a)(2) and the state's certificate of title statute direct the secured creditor to perfect by

---

1   In New York, secured parties file the UCC-1 financing statements with the Division of Corporations, State Records, and UCC. See http://www.dos.ny.gov/corps/euccfilingguide.html (last visited Nov. 7 2016).

2   The general rule—filing a financing statement—protects a secured creditor's interest in the deposit account only if the deposit account is proceeds of collateral, per UCC §§ 9–102 & 9–315.

3   UCC §§ 9–312 & 9–313.

noting its lien on the vehicle's certificate of title.[4] Likewise, if the Prius is consumer goods—used by the debtor for personal, family or household purposes—then Article 9 also requires that a secured party perfect by noting its lien on the car's certificate of title.[5]

But if the Prius is inventory—as when the debtor is a car dealer or car rental company—then the UCC§9–311 exception does not apply. Instead, §9–311 (d) directs the secured creditor back to the general rule of filing a UCC-1 under §9–310 to perfect.

In short, when you come across collateral that is a motor vehicle, start by determining whether it's inventory, equipment, or consumer goods. If it is inventory, UCC § 9–311 tells a secured party to perfect in the general way, by filing a financing statement. If instead the vehicle is equipment or consumer goods, the secured party should perfect by noting its lien on the certificate of title.

Which classification fits for the truck used by the Store to transport inventory and equipment?

By this point of the course you should have immediately answered "equipment." Accordingly, the next task is to comply with the New York certificate of title statute.

2. Perfecting by Complying with a Certificate of Title Statute

As a preliminary matter, make sure that the certificate of title statute governs the transaction. The Store's truck is covered by the Certificate of Title Statute because it is a motor vehicle that operates on highways.[6]

---

4   See Uniform Motor Vehicle Certificate of Title and Anti-Theft Act § 20 (2006).

5   This certificate of title rule applies even for purchase money security interests in vehicles that are consumer goods, because the automatic perfection rule for PMSIs in consumer goods explicitly excludes motor vehicles. UCC §9–309(1). Similarly, a security interest in an aircraft that is consumer goods can only be perfected by following the Federal Aviation Act's requirements.

6   McKinney's Laws of NY Vehicle & Traffic Law §§2101 (n), 159 & 2250 (2016). Together these sections provide that the Certificate of Title law applies to motor vehicles operated on highways as well as water-

The next step is to determine how to comply with the statutory requirement. Section 2118(b)(1) of New York's Certificate of Title Act provides in relevant part:

"A security interest is perfected:

(A) By the delivery to the commissioner of (i) the existing certificate of title, if any, an application for a certificate of title containing the name and address of the lienholder and the required fee...; [and]

(B) As of the time of its creation if the delivery is completed within ten days thereafter, otherwise, as of the time of the delivery."[7]

Accordingly FNB must get the certificate of title on the truck and apply to have its name listed on it within ten days of the security interest attaching. Here is the certificate of title:

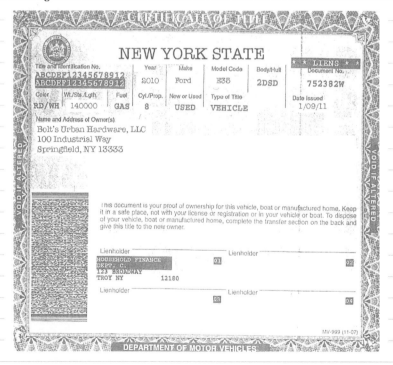

---

craft and mobile homes, but not to human-powered means of transport like bicycles nor to railroad cars.

7   McKinney's Laws of NY Vehicle & Traffic Law § 2118 (2016).

And here is the Notice of Lien form that New York requires creditors to fill out and submit with a $5.00 fee to be perfected:

MV-900 (1/11)   New York State Department of Motor Vehicles

NOTICE OF LIEN

www.dmv.ny.gov

All information (other than signature) must be typed. Use caution when entering Vehicle, Hull or Manufactured Home ID number. Liens will not be recorded if information is illegible, incorrect or incomplete.

VEHICLE/BOAT/MANUFACTURED HOME INFORMATION

Identification Number			
Year	Make	Body Type/Hull	Registration/Plate No. of Borrower, if any
This is a: ☐ Vehicle	☐ Boat	☐ Trailer	☐ Manufactured Home

OWNER INFORMATION

Owner's Last Name	First	M.I.
Owner's Last Name	First	M.I.
Street Address (including Apt. No.)		
City	State	Zip Code

☐ Check here if this is a new address.

NOTE: Lien will be recorded only if the name(s) listed as the owner(s) is EXACTLY the same as the owner(s) recorded, or to be recorded, on the Certificate of Title. If a Certificate of Title has not been issued to this borrower, print the name as it appears on the driver license.

OWNER'S STATEMENT: I understand that the lienholder will send this notice to the DEPARTMENT OF MOTOR VEHICLES. If a title was previously issued in my name for this vehicle, boat, trailer or manufactured home, I gave it to the lienholder to be sent to DMV with this notice. I understand that a new Certificate of Title, showing the lienholder's name, will be mailed to me.

OWNER(S): SIGN HERE ⇨ _____ ⇨ _____ Date _____

(Must be an original signature. If a POA is used, a copy of the POA must be attached.)

If signing for a corporation, print your name and title:

_____   _____

(Name)   (Title)

LIEN INFORMATION

Lien Filing Code (assigned by the DMV: enter only if a code has been assigned to you or your company)		
Lienholder's Name		
Lienholder's Name (continued)		
Street Address		
City	State	Zip Code

This notice authorizes the Department of Motor Vehicles to disclose (or otherwise make available) information about the lienholder obtained by the department in connection with this record.

⇨ _____ Date of Security Agreement _____

   (Lienholder's Signature—Must be an original signature or a facsimile stamp)

Has a NY Certificate of Title been issued to this borrower? ☐ YES ☐ NO *IF YES, ATTACH TITLE.*

LIENHOLDER: Mail this form, the $5 fee ***paid by the lienholder*** payable to the Commissioner of Motor Vehicles, and the owner's title (if issued) to: TITLE BUREAU, NEW YORK STATE DEPARTMENT OF MOTOR VEHICLES, PO BOX 2604, ALBANY NY 12220-0604

You can verify online if a lien was recorded or if a title certificate was issued. Go to the Lien/Title Certificate Status page at the DMV web site: **www.dmv.ny.gov/titlestat/ default.html**

The certificate of title and Notice of Lien form are downloadable from book website. You will fill out the Notice of Lien and print out both documents to complete the student assignment in Part II.

Next, we turn to fixtures, another type of collateral that has an exceptional priority rule as well as perfection rules governed by statutes other than Article 9.

B. Fixtures

Because fixtures exist on the boundary between real and personal property, both perfection and priority of this kind of collateral requires a close read of Article 9 and real property laws. We will focus on Article 9's distinction between filings regarding fixtures in the UCC-1 files and "fixture filings," which a secured party files in the separate system for perfecting security interests in land.

1. Definitions and Scope

UCC §9–102 defines a fixture as "goods that have become so related to particular real property that an interest in them arises under real property law." It also defines "fixture filings" as "the filing of a financing statement covering goods that are or are to become fixtures and satisfying Section 9–502(a) and (b)."

Before seeing how a UCC-1 filing regarding fixtures differs from a "fixture filing," we must be sure that Article 9 governs. At first glance, you may think that fixtures are not Article 9 collateral since §9–109(d) (11) excludes from Article 9 coverage "the creation or transfer of an interest in or lien on real property." But that section also carves out an exception to that general rule: Under §9–109(d)(11)(B) and (C) both fixtures and fixture filings are covered by Article 9.[8]

Now we have sufficient information to determine whether the shelves, awnings, lighting, and display cases in the Store are fixtures.

The short answer is that fixtures are personal property that is closely associated with land. As Professor Steve Knippenberg put it, "You take the world, you shake it, and everything that doesn't fall off is a fixture."[9] But states have different rules defining precisely what is and is not a fixture, so it can be hard for a creditor to know with certainty whether the collateral is a fixture. For purposes of this exercise we will assume that the shelves, awnings, and other things attached to the Store's walls, ceiling and floor are fixtures.

2. Perfecting a Security Interest in Fixtures

Now we must determine how to perfect a security interest in those fixtures. FNB can use two methods, one that protects it against more competitors than the other.

UCC §9–501(b) allows a creditor to file a financing statement in the Article 9 files or to record the interest in the real estate records. Comment 4 to that section explains that choice and the difference in terminology between a filing in the UCC files and one in the records for encumbrances on real property:

> "There are two ways in which a secured party may file a financing statement to perfect a security interest in goods that are to become

---

8   §9–109(d)(11)(D) also provides that Article 9 governs "security agreements covering personal and real property" per § 9–604, and § 9–604 in turn states that when a security interest covers fixtures, the secured party may proceed under either Article 9 or real property law. In contrast, a retail tenant's interest in a real estate lease—such as the Store's interest in its lease of the premises in which it operates Bolt's Urban Hardware—is excluded from Article 9 coverage under 9–109(d)(11). An exception is that some jurisdictions treat an interest in a co-op apartment as Article 9 collateral. Lawrence R. Ahern III, 1 *The Law of Debtors and Creditors* §7:41 (2016).

9   Lynn M. LoPucki, Elizabeth Warren & Robert M. Lawless, *Secured Credit* 347 (8th ed. 2016).

fixtures. It may file in the Article 9 records, as with most other goods. . . . Or it may file the financing statement as a "fixture filing" defined by 9–102 in the office in which a record of a mortgage on the related real property would be filed."

In other words, "fixture filing" is a term of art for a secured party's filing in the real property records. Creditors may do that or file a UCC-1 financing statement with the Secretary of State or other office that accepts financing statements regarding personal property.

That choice between filing offices sounds easy enough until you realize that §9–502(b) requires a fixture filing to include more than §9–502(a)'s bare-bones elements of debtor's name, creditor's name and an identification of the collateral. Under §9–502(b), the fixture filing must meet four additional requirements:

1. Indicate that it covers this type of collateral;

2. Indicate that it is to be filed in the real property records;

3. Provide a description of the real property to which the collateral is related sufficient to give constructive notice of a mortgage under the law . . . if the description were contained in a . . . mortgage of the real property; and

4. If the debtor does not have an interest of record in the real property, provide the name of the record owner.

Items #3 and #4 on this list pose two challenges.

First, the standard for describing the real property for a mortgage is much more stringent than UCC §§9–108 and 9–504's minimal requirement of identifying the thing described. FNB would have to find the tract of property on which the building is located in the records of the county in which it is located (including the book in which it is located, and the relevant page).[10] Second, the lender may not know who owns the real property, or may have the wrong name.

Here, the debtor Bolt's Urban Hardware, LLC does not own the building, and thus FNB would have to find out the person or entity that does own it. Given the expense and time of tracking down that information—and confirming its accuracy—FNB could rationally conclude that making a fixture filing in the real property records is sufficiently burdensome that the better approach is to file a financing statement in the UCC-1 files.

However, FMB should know that a UCC-1 filing could carry an additional cost.

3. Priority between UCC-1 and Fixture Filing

Under §9–334(c) a creditor who takes the time, trouble and expense of filing in the real property records has priority over competing creditors who filed in the Article 9 files. UCC § 9–334 provides some exceptions not relevant to the fixtures at Bolt's Urban Hardware, such as readily removable office machines and purchase money security interests, so the general rule of priority between a UCC-1 covering fixtures and a fixture filing in the real property records could result in FNB losing a priority contest to the fixtures with a creditor who did file in the real property records.

But this conclusion does not end your inquiry. While a UCC-1 financing statement filed in the Secretary of State's office with other financing statements would be primed by a creditor who made a fixture filing, that UCC-1 creditor could still prevail over other claims. Most important is §9–334(e) (3)'s provision that a creditor perfected in the UCC-1 files has priority over lien creditors such as the bankruptcy trustee. Official Comment 9 to §9–334 explains that priority scheme:

---

10   LoPucki, Warren & Lawless, *Secured Credit* 344–345 (8th ed. 2016).

"Judgment creditors generally are not reliance creditors who search real-property records. Accordingly, a perfected fixture security interest takes priority over a subsequent judgment lien or other lien obtained by legal or equitable proceedings, even if no evidence of the security interest appears in the relevant real-property records."

Because perfected secured creditors generally take priority over lien creditors and the bankruptcy trustee has the rights of a lien creditor, the Comment concludes that this provision gives a perfected fixture security interest priority over claims by a trustee in bankruptcy.[11]

4. Strategy: UCC-1 or Fixture Filing?

Now that you know how to perfect a fixture filing in the real property records, and the priority relationship between a fixture filing and a filing that covers fixtures in the UCC-1 files for personal property, how do you advise your client to proceed?

Consider the expense of compiling a fixture filing, including your fees, and the likelihood of a priority contest with a real property owner or encumbrancer regarding the shelves, awnings, lighting, and display cases in the Store.

Many secured creditors in FNB's position would conclude that it is quick and easy—and accordingly inexpensive—to ensure that the financing statement and security agreement perfect FNB's interest in the fixtures within the UCC-1 files. Moreover, the payoff from perfecting through a fixture filing in the real property records seems unlikely to be worth the effort. Most debtors pay their debts, and you could spend some time—and your client's money—to search the real-property fillies only to discover that another creditor already has priority over any interest that FNB could assert. Finally, those fixtures may not be valuable enough to justify all that effort and expense.

---

11   *See* UCC §9–317.

Accordingly, assume for the student assignment below that Lamar Lee, on behalf of FNB, instructs you to protect the bank's priority over the bankruptcy trustee and others with lien creditor status, but not to bother with a fixture filing.

Part II: Student Assignment

A. Perfection of Truck

Download a copy of the Notice of Lien from the book website. Fill it out with the information about the truck listed on the certificate of title on page 239. Assume that the registration plate is 54111-ME

B. Perfection of Fixtures

Review your security agreement from exercise #4 and the financing statement from exercise #3 to make sure that the collateral description in both documents covers the shelves, awnings, lighting, and display cases in the Store. Make any changes necessary to ensure attachment and perfection.

C. Tips for the Exercise

❑ Re: the truck

❑ Follow instructions on the form, which include attaching a copy of the certificate if title.

❑ Pass in both documents.

❑ Re: fixtures

❑ Pass in your financing statement and the collateral description in your security agreement. Because the only relevant language for the security agreement is the collateral description, your professor may simply require that you provide that clause.

D. Checklist

❑ Proofread Notice of Lien, triple checking the VIN

❑ Sign the Notice of Lien

❑ Pass in both CoT and Notice of Lien

❑ Make sure that any after-acquired clause covers fixtures description in security agreement

Creating the Portfolio and Client Cover Letter

Skill: Client Communication & Document Integration

Overview

This exercise brings together the previous exercises by having you put together all of the documents that you have drafted into a portfolio that you would send to your client, accompanied by a cover letter or memo.

Part I explains the format and substance of client letters and memos. Part II provides detailed instructions on how to properly combine the documents into one coherent package, including ways to ensure that they properly reference one another. In Part III—the student assignment—you draft that cover letter or memo and create the portfolio that includes the security agreement, promissory note, certificate of title, notice of lien, financing statement, and personal guaranty.

Part I: Client Memos & Letters Explained

As we saw in exercise #8 on professional ethics, lawyers must communicate regularly with their clients. Determining the right format and substance for those communications requires complying with conventions of professionalism and making sure to write clearly and briefly. A typo or other sloppiness in your client communications could shake your client's faith in your expertise and diligence in the transaction as a whole.

Client memoranda and letters serve many purposes. They can describe business or legal issues that arise during negotiation and drafting, explain how an issue was resolved, describe a problem and propose a solution, report on the progress of negotiation or drafting, or seek client guidance on matters such as strategy. For this exercise assume that the attorneys and the parties have resolved all substantive issues regarding the financed purchase of Bolt's Urban Hardware, LLC, and that you are sending your client a copy of the completed, executed documents along with a cover letter or memo explaining the contents.

Remember to write clearly and succinctly, with minimum use of legalese, since your clients likely are not lawyers and in any case will judge your work by the quality of your emails, letters, and other communications. Format the material in a way that facilitates quick and easy comprehension, and do not waste your client's time with minor issues. Though substantive memos about the details of relevant legal rules must of necessity go into more detail, this exercise has you practice with the simplest content that a lawyer sends to his client.

Your firm or client may prefer more formal communication through hard-copy letters sent through the mail, or less formal memos sent as attachments to email. Generally speaking, legal practice has moved toward almost exclusive use of electronic versions of documents, including e-filing in federal courts.

When attorneys attach a letter sent electronically to an email message, they can either include the substance of a memo in the body of the email and attach any relevant documents, or have the memo be an attachment and say in the email "please see the attached memorandum and attachments." One seasoned government lawyer reports that she prefers to attach the memo as a document because it seems more likely that the memo and attachments will be printed out and stored or filed together. Rather than send documents in Word—which can be easily altered—lawyers generally send the documents in PDF, and scrub the metadata before conversion. Attorneys tend to send a Word document only when they seek comments or edits back from the recipient, but even then they scrub the metadata before pressing "send."

Because letters and memos follow different formats, we address each in turn.

A. Letter to the Client

Though attorneys rarely communicate by hard-copy letters, many continue to use the format of a letter, which is then scanned into a PDF and sent as an attachment to email. Here is a sample format[1]

Hutz & Hutz
Springfield Mall | Springfield, NY 13333

November 29, 2017

Confidential Attorney-Client Communication

Via Electronic Mail

Lamar Lee
Vice President of Commercial Lending
First National Bank of Springfield
700 N. Burns St.
Springfield Heights, NY 13333
llee@email.com

Re: Executed Documents in Financed Purchase of Bolt's Urban Hardware, LLC

---

1   Based on Michelle M. Harner, *Developing Professional Skills: Business Associations* 55–57 (2013).

Dear Mr. Lee,

[Substance of the letter]

We have also retained copies for our files. Please do not hesitate to call me with any questions or comments.

Sincerely,

_____

[Attorney Name]

Note the notice of confidentiality at the top of the letter. Any client communication should protect the privileged information contained in the letter or email. While letters often have a simple four-word notice of the attorney-client communications, emails generally have a longer, standardized statement designating the material as privileged and warning others not to read it. The difference may be due to the ease with which email is forwarded, often including prior messages in a chain. A typical email provision reads as follows:

"**CONFIDENTIALITY NOTICE.** The information contained in this email message and any attachments is ATTORNEY PRIVILEGED AND CONFIDENTIAL INFORMATION intended only for the use of the individual or entity named herein. If you are not the intended recipient or the employee or agent responsible for delivering it to the intended recipient, you are hereby notified that any dissemination, distribution or copying of this communication is prohibited. If you have received this communication in error, please immediately notify Hutz & Hutz at (718) 555-5299 or by reply email and delete the original message and any attachments. Thank you for your cooperation."

Just as attorneys and clients prefer the speed and informality of email over hard-copy letters, they increasingly communicate by the more informal method of memos.

B. Memo to the Client

Sometimes lawyers write their memos to their clients in the body of an email, and sometimes they create a Word document and then attach it to the email. If you create a separate memo, use a format that includes lines for "To," "From," "Date," and "Re," the subject matter of the memo. For example:

To:	Bianca Bolt
From:	Leslie Lawstudent
Date:	November 29, 2017
Re:	Documents for Bolt's Urban Hardware Financing Transaction

As with a letter or email, be sure to note that the memo is covered by attorney/client and work product confidentiality protections. The top of the memo might provide in all caps, bold font **"PRIVILEGED AND CONFIDENTIAL: ATTORNEY CLIENT WORK PRODUCT,"** or contain a watermark across the text indicating those protections. Insert a line across the page to separate the heading from the body of the memo.

Begin the memo with an introductory paragraph explaining the contents. Increase readability by making the memo single spaced with blank lines between paragraphs. Remember that your client will judge the contents by the cover memo and that a single typo or missing word invites a reader to question the writer's abilities and diligence. Use your spell check function and also proof-read carefully.

Organize a memo covering an ethical issue or question of strategic choices based on your legal research with numbered headings and put your conclusion right after the introduction to quickly inform your time-pressed client of the results of your research and any proposed action you suggest. In a longer memo with multiple points, put the headline up front in a topic sentence at the beginning of each section.

For this exercise you are providing the client and Bianca Bolt as personal guarantor with copies of the final executed documents for their files, so you need only recap the transaction in a sentence or two and list the documents that accompany the memo. Bullet points efficiently disclose the contents of the package for the person you are sending them to and to anyone else pulling the papers from the file months or years from when you send them.

Problem 10: Client Email

Evaluate the following excerpts from an attorney's email to her client.

- **At the end of text of email:** "That's all. Have a fantastic holiday weekend!! ☺"

- **Subject line reads:** "Contracts" & text of email reads "FYI"

- **Subject line reads:** "Closing on Bolt's Urban Hardware Financing" and text is several screens long, beginning with the following text: "Dear Mr. Lee, Attached hereto are the documents executed as part and parcel of the Purchase of Bolt's Urban Hardware, LLC, located at 100 Industrial Way, Springfield, NY, 1333, which company is formed under the laws of the State of New York . . . "

Part II: Creating a Transactional Portfolio

Over the course of this book you have drafted three distinct agreements—the promissory note, the security agreement and the personal guaranty—and two supporting documents to perfect FNB's security interest in the collateral: the financing statement and the notice of lien on the debtor's truck. We conclude by compiling these documents to work as an integrated whole, packaged as it would be to a client. As a bonus this portfolio should work as a writing sample to show a potential employer the negotiation and drafting skills that you have developed in this course.

A. Creating an Integrated Portfolio

Drafters create a portfolio in two stages. First they review the substance of the documents, and then they put them together to create a formal record of the transaction. We cover each in turn and end with a checklist.

1. One Last Review[2]

The drafter must ask, "Is this document going to work?" Will it serve the client's objectives effectively, efficiently, and without the need to resort to litigation?" The drafter should review the document several times, from a different perspectives: one that focuses on substantive provisions; and another that focuses on the document's structure; and finally weeding out the ever-hard-to-spot typos.

Some of the items on the review list below involve "vertical review," requiring the drafter to look in depth at each provision for hidden ambiguities and stylistic flaws. Other items on the list involve "horizontal review," requiring the drafter to compare how a particular topic is handled in different provisions throughout the document and among the documents that make up a transaction.

---

2   Based on Haggard & Kuney, *Legal Drafting* 354–55 (2nd ed. 2007).

When reviewing documents drafted by others, and when critically examining your own drafting, focus your review on the following:

- **Parties, Dates, Dollar Amounts, and Interest Rates.**

Does the document identify the correct parties in their proper capacities? Are the dates correct? Are all currency amounts and interest rates correct and complete? Never assume that any factual statement is correct. Trust, but verify.

- **Appropriate Structure.**

Do the document and the overall structure of the transaction suit your client's needs? Do you understand the deal that is at issue? Does the document match your client's expectations? Does it match your client's earlier description of the deal to you?

- **Clear Expression of Duties & Privileges.**

Does the document's mandatory duty provisions clear regarding all performances by other parties? Are mandatory duties specified using the words "shall" or "must?" Are rights or privileges expressed in terms of "is entitled to" and privileges in terms of "may?" Do these provisions clearly state who does what to or for whom or what, when? Timing of performance is essential. Be sure to specify the "when."

- **Representations and Warranties.**

Does the document contain representations and warranties running in favor of your client regarding all facts, statements, and assurances upon which your client is relying? Are any qualifiers (knowledge or materiality) appropriate? Are your client's representations and warranties factually correct? How about those of the other side? Are there any that you know to be false?

· **Internal and External Consistency.**

Does the document fit the desired structure? Is it complete and consistent, internally and with any other documents involved in the transaction? Defined terms and boilerplate should be consistent across all documents in a transaction to avoid confusion and potential ambiguity. Are all of the documents governed by the same notice, integration, choice of law, choice of forum, and alternative dispute resolution provisions?

· **Substantive Understanding.**

Do you understand each provision of the document? Review each of them until you understand it completely and its interaction with the other sections of the document and related documents.

· **Hypothesize Performance.**

Think through the life of the transaction and the documents under various fact patterns. What will happen, moment by moment, if the parties comply with all the terms in a timely manner? Are performances required in the proper order?

· **Hypothesize Non-Performance and Default.**

What if one or both parties fail to perform all or part of the agreement? Are the consequences of failure of conditions or failure to perform stated and closely linked to the performance required? Are the events of default and associated remedies clear? Capitalize on the opportunity to prevent trouble before it occurs.

· **Prepare a Summary.**

Summarize the document provision-by-provision. If the drafter finds it difficult to summarize the content of the document, the document likely will be even more incomprehensible to a reader who is not already familiar with it. Writing a summary may also reveal discrepancies. This summary could be the basis of the cover memo to the client.

2. Exhibits

Exhibits are documents that are appended to the end of the agreement and often incorporated in it by reference. Some drafting experts see the "incorporated by reference" language as unnecessary since courts generally treat a sufficiently specific reference to the document as incorporating it by reference, as long as the parties know the document's terms or can easily access them. To be safe, however, many drafters include a statement of incorporation.

Some drafters create a free-standing declaration that all exhibits are incorporated by reference, as follows:

> ***Incorporation by Reference.*** *Every exhibit, schedule and other appendix attached to this Agreement and is incorporated in this Agreement by reference.*

Another approach incorporates each document by reference when you first refer to it. For example:

> *Debtor has executed the promissory note dated November 22, 2017, for the principal amount of $700,000 (**"Note"**), which is attached as Exhibit A and incorporated here by reference.*

This language contemplates—and requires—that the note be physically attached to the security agreement. While that task is easy in the transaction between FNB and Bolt's Urban Hardware, LLC, in other transactions an exhibit may be too voluminous to be easily attached. In that situation, the drafter should omit the "which is attached" reference.

Remember that incorporation is a one-way street. In the transaction between FNB and Bolt's Urban Hardware, the security agreement should incorporate by reference the note and the personal guaranty. That process does not incorporate the security agreement into the note. If it did, then the note might become non-negotiable because it would contain all the conditions in the security agreement and thus violate the rule that negotiable instruments must be unconditional promises to pay money. Thus incorporation becomes a bit more complex when you seek to incorporate the note and security agreement into the personal guaranty, and the note and personal guaranty into the security agreement.

Consider the security agreement. You could incorporate it by reference in the personal guaranty in two ways. You could attach it to the personal guaranty as Exhibit 1, but that seems bulky and duplicative. In the alternative, you could adapt the standard language of incorporation by reference to incorporate by reference the security agreement to which the personal guaranty is attached as an exhibit. For example,

> *"**Security Agreement**" means the Security Agreement executed between Debtor and Lender on November 22, 2017, to which this Personal Guaranty is attached as Exhibit B, and which is incorporated here by reference.*

Another variation of incorporation and exhibits occurs when parties enter a letter of intent—also known as a memorandum of understanding or "MOU"—before the transaction is finalized. If a transaction closes a month or two after initial documents are signed, then the initial documents could attach an unsigned version of the note and security agreement as exhibits and the debtor would sign the documents at the time of closing. That kind of provision could read as follows:

> *At or before Closing, Debtor shall execute the promissory note dated November 22, 2017, for the principal amount of $700,000 (**"Note"**), substantially in the form of **Exhibit A** and incorporated here by reference.*

Note that "**Exhibit A**" is in bold font. Some drafters use bold font the first time they reference an exhibit to make it easy to find on the page. The "substantially in the form" language allows the actual note that the debtor signs to have minor differences from the one attached to the preliminary document. For example, the parties may fill in the date on the day of closing. At the closing the attorneys would fill the proper date, delete the title "Exhibit A" from the note, and the debtor would sign it.

Drafters label exhibits sequentially, such as Exhibit A, Exhibit B, and so on. If an exhibit has its own exhibits, drafters use an alternate method of designating the sequence. In the transaction between FNB and Bolt's Urban Hardware, exhibits to the security agreement could be labeled A, B, and C, and an exhibit to the personal guaranty would then be labeled Exhibit 1.

3. Cascade Issues

Make sure that your general provisions, so-called boilerplate, are consistent. If the security agreement requires that modifications be memorialized in signed writings, make sure that the note and personal guaranty have the same language. Otherwise incorporating the documents will create ambiguity about what modifications are enforceable, and by whom.

Along the same lines, make sure that your integration, choice of law and other interpretative and endgame clauses are consistent across the documents.

Now you are ready to do the student assignment.

III. Student Assignment: Cover Letter & Portfolio

Review and edit your security agreement, note, and personal guaranty, as well as the notice of lien and financing statement to incorporate comments by your instructor and materials covered in class since you completed that assignment. Compile them with exhibit pages indicating the function of the note, personal guaranty and other documents as attachments to the security agreement.

Write a cover letter or memo that you will send to your client along with a complete set of the executed documents. You have worked in pairs but only need to write to a single client, so pick one client and address the memo or letter to that client. Remember that Bianca Bolt is also individually liable under the personal guaranty, so that she should get full set of the documents as well. Rather than write two letters, you can say in your letter or memo that you have also sent these documents to Bianca Bolt at her home address.

You can attach the supporting documents—financing statement and notice of lien—in two ways. Either make them exhibits to the security agreement, or personal guaranty, as appropriate, or enclose them with the memo as additional supporting materials. If you take the later course, list the financing statement and notice of liens after the security agreement and its exhibits.

A. Drafting Tips:

❏ Mark the letter or memo as privileged attorney/client communication

❏ List the documents with bullet points

❏ Mention that you are retaining originals for your files

❏ Say that you are also sending a complete set of the documents to opposing counsel and to Bianca Bolt in her individual capacity as guarantor

❏ Explain what the lender's counsel has done to ensure that the security interest is perfected

B. Checklist

General: Check that all documents

❏ Reflect negotiated terms

❏ Cover all relevant facts

❏ Work together

❏ Use defined terms consistently

❏ Use cross-references correctly

❏ Are clear, concise & well organized

❏ Inform the reader of parties' rights & duties

C. Compiling the Portfolio

❏ Security agreement as "envelope"

❏ Note & personal guaranty as exhibits

❏ Exhibits incorporated in security agreement by reference

❏ Personal guaranty incorporates note and security agreement by reference

❏ Consistent boilerplate

❏ Consistency across documents (i.e., FNB is "Lender" in all documents)

❏ Cover memo or letter

    ❏ protects client confidentiality

    ❏ briefly describes transaction documents

    ❏ brief describes method of perfection

    ❏ states that Bianca gets an additional copy of the documents for herself personally if the portfolio includes her guaranty.

• SKILL: CLIENT COMMUNICATION & DOCUMENT INTEGRATION